MORE THAN
GLUE & GLITTER

MORE THAN GLUE & GLITTER

A CLASSROOM GUIDE FOR VOLUNTEER TEACHERS

by Debbie Trafton O'Neal

AUGSBURG ● MINNEAPOLIS

MORE THAN GLUE AND GLITTER
A Classroom Guide for Volunteer Teachers

Cover and interior design: RKB Studios, Inc.

Library of Congress Cataloging-in-Publication Data

O'Neal, Debbie Trafton.
    More than glue and glitter : a classroom guide for volunteer
teachers / Debbie Trafton O'Neal.
      p.   cm.
    ISBN 0-8066-2561-9 (alk. paper)
    1. Christian education of children.   2. Christian education—
Teaching methods.   I. Title.
BV1475.2.045 1992
268'.432—dc20
                                                        91-47157
                                                        CIP

The paper used in this publication meets the minimum requirements of American National Standard for Information Sciences—Permanence of Paper for Printed Library Materials, ANSI Z329.48-1984. ∞™

Manufactured in the U.S.A.   AF 9-2561
96   6   7   8   9   10

This book is dedicated to students and teachers everywhere, especially to those who volunteer their time, talents, and energy in the area of Christian education, and with special thanks to the teachers, friends, and Parish Education Committee at Grace Lutheran Church in Des Moines, Washington.

93511

CONTENTS

Preface 9

Chapter 1   Understanding How Children
Learn 11

Age-level characteristics 11
Faith development in children 17

Chapter 2   Creating a Climate for
Learning 21

Climate indicators 21
Arranging your classroom 22
Display space 25
Making contact with students 28
Involving families 29
Involving the congregation 30

Chapter 3   Classroom Management 31

Success and responsibility 31
Rules for keeping peace 32
Attention getters and boredom beaters 33
Discipline in the classroom 35
Correcting behavior problems 39

Chapter 4   Every Child Is a Child of God 41

Fostering self-esteem 41
Activities that build self-esteem 42
Motivation 45
Involving children who have special needs 46

Chapter 5   Successful Teaching Techniques 53

Preparing the lesson 54
Learning styles/teaching styles 60
Learning activities and materials 61
Teaching options 66

Chapter 6   Telling God's Story 69

Storytelling 69
Using your memory 72

Chapter 7   Creative, Hands-On Learning   73

Art projects 73
Creative writing 81
Drama 83
Music in the classroom 85
Evangelism and outreach 88
Worship in the classroom 89

In Conclusion 93

At the many workshops and teacher training events in which I have participated over the past twelve years, the same issues and concerns seem to crop up. From Wyoming to North Dakota, Oregon to British Columbia, I found that teachers and education leaders ask the same questions.

How can I make the most of my teaching time of an hour (or less)? What are some good organizational skills I can incorporate into my classroom? What are the best ways to keep students' interest? How should we discipline within the church school setting? How can I, someone who is not a biblical scholar, share the truths of God's Word in ways that will make a difference to my students?

It was these questions, along with many others, that prompted me to write this book. The more I heard these questions repeated, the more I thought there ought to be a practical, usable resource for those teachers who share God's Word in Sunday school and vacation Bible school classrooms.

The title *More Than Glue and Glitter* reflects my own philosophy of the education process in church-related programs today. There *is* more to teaching Sunday school or vacation Bible school than fun art projects or singing time around a piano. And you don't have to be a professionally trained teacher to know and to understand some of the basic elements of the education process. In fact, once you know some of these basic pieces to the puzzle of education, you will be equipped to create an enthusiasm for learning in your classroom. It is my hope that this book will help you do just that!

Before you can begin to teach, you need to know some things about your students. A positive teaching and learning experience depends on being prepared to enter the classroom. This chapter deals with the expectations you might have of your students, and the actual levels of learning they can achieve.

Age-level characteristics for children ages two to fourteen

Children learn in different ways at different stages of mental and physical development. What works for a ten-year-old child may not work for a three-year-old. How you teach needs to reflect your students' ability to learn. By taking age-level characteristics into consideration, you will have a better idea of what kinds of things to look for in your students and what kinds of learning activities will work best in the classroom. The following section gives general information on age-level characteristics. If you wish to learn more, many excellent resources are available that give a more detailed outline.

Although most churches offer some sort of nursery program for their youngest members, it seems the earliest age when children enter the classroom is age two. This is the reason I have chosen to begin with children who are two years old. Other ages are broken down according to the way that church schools and curriculum are commonly grouped.

As with any set of developmental characteristics, these will vary from child to child.

In addition, the last paragraph of each age-level section gives a brief look into where children of each particular age may fit into the stages of faith development. There is more information on faith development in the section following this.

Two-year-olds

If you have two-year-old children in a church school classroom, this may well be the first encounter they have with a group setting.

A two-year-old child is energetic and has a short attention span. Although the rest of the group may be engaged in a new activity, the two-year-old child may not want to stop what he or she is doing to join in. Once a routine in the classroom has been established, the two-year-old child will expect that routine to be repeated. Although sometimes it is necessary to vary a classroom routine, it is best to avoid doing this with two-year-olds.

Two-year-olds are egocentric in their responses within a classroom, and they will each have a different way of letting you know what their needs are. For some children, this will mean crying. For others, expressing their needs will take the form of hitting or grabbing the object they want. If possible, it is helpful to observe the children for one or two sessions with limited group activities to get a good idea of each child's unique personality.

As children become older twos, their motor skills and cognitive development increase remarkably. Most two-year-olds can hold a crayon correctly, build a tower of six blocks or more, match colors and shapes, unbutton their coats (but not button), and begin to catch and throw balls or beanbags.

Older two-year-olds have increased cognitive and intellectual abilities as well. Symbols begin to have meaning and the children can identify and use them correctly. Older two-year-olds can begin to recall details and repeat them, although not always in accurate order. An increased attention span is also an important point to remember for older twos, although they still need short periods of activity followed by a different activity or a rest.

A teacher of two-year-olds will see a big difference in language skills and development as the year progresses. Children will begin to ask questions related to the content you are teaching. They will begin to use plurals and complex questions that label their thoughts and actions.

Two-year-olds can learn the names for God and Jesus. They will recognize and identify concrete religious items often represented by symbols, such as a star, the cross, a church, or baby Jesus. Older two-year-olds will also realize that prayer is talking to God, the Bible is a special book that tells about God and God's people, and that some behavior is appropriate and some is not.

Three- and four-year-olds

If your church does not offer classes for two-year-olds, the class for three- and four-year-olds will most likely be a first group experience. A predictable, logical routine of activities will help these preschoolers feel comfortable in the classroom. Your acceptance of their different personalities and interests will make them feel loved and accepted both by you and by God.

Three- and four-year-olds have immense amounts of energy, and their curiosity is part of their charm. Both of these qualities, however, translate into short attention spans and a need for simple, specific directions. Be concise and specific for all directions, whether they involve making a craft project or explaining how to line up to use the rest room.

Repetition is one of the most common ways of learning for the three- and four-year-old child. This does not mean drilling a child on a particular subject, but incorporating a Bible verse, song, or thought into the entire learning experience for that day. It is also helpful to review the material the next time you meet with the children.

A rule of thumb is to remember that three- and four-year-old children have an attention span of about ten minutes. Any activities should be geared to this time frame, alternating quiet and active times whenever possible.

Sharing with others is becoming a concept that is understood but not always liked by children this age. Group interaction and social skills are being tentatively tried out in small groups within the larger group. Be aware of this and help the children make choices and decisions that will not hurt others, but that will foster their own social skills.

Children who are three or four years old think of Jesus as their friend. They are beginning to sense God's part in the created world around them, and they learn about God through stories. They are very loving and will learn best what it means to be a Christian by imitating others.

Five- and six-year-olds

Working with children who are five and six is a delightful experience. These children are eager to belong to a group and they have fun together laughing about whatever they think is silly at the moment! They most likely have been involved in other group situations and will adjust quite easily to being a part of the group in the classroom. It is still important to offer a clear, predictable routine within the classroom. Everyone benefits when they know what to expect and what is expected of them, but children with special needs will especially appreciate some regular routine or order to class time.

Almost all five- and six-year-olds enjoy learning. These children will have longer attention spans and will participate readily in discussion and activities that relate to the Bible story or other learning. It is still wise to alternate quiet and active times within the class session, although not as many are needed as with younger children.

Five- and six-year-olds are becoming more and more independent, but they still may need adult help with some activities. Some children's large motor skills will be very well-developed at this time while their fine motor skills are somewhat behind. With little observation, you will be able to note the children who need help with particular skills and can help them unobtrusively without embarrassing them in front of their peers. These children may seem very emotional at times and will need your acceptance and calm voice to help them understand their feelings.

Children in this age group continue to learn the most about God through other people. Relationships help them see what unique people they are and help them to understand how the members of God's family of believers share love with one another. Your acceptance, patience, and respect for each child as an individual will play a major part in building his or her self-esteem. Stories about Jesus and learning to pray will help children better understand their own relationship with God.

Whenever possible, it is important for these children to learn parts of the worship service so that they can participate fully when they attend worship. This, above all else, will give them a true sense of belonging to the community of believers.

First and second graders

Church school can be an important part of first and second graders' lives. Because these children have been in a school setting before, they adjust easily to a routine that the teacher establishes. A sense of belonging is extremely important to children this age, and you will want to note if all the children in your class attend the same school during the week. If they do not, you may want to plan special "getting to know you" activities within the sessions you teach. Although this age of children enjoys working in groups, be aware of those who prefer to work independently and offer opportunities for them to do so.

Because children in the first and second grades have begun to read and write, there will be more ways to involve them within the classroom. However, be careful not to spend too much time using books, pencils, and paper. Also, be aware of children who may feel self-conscious about reading aloud. Don't force them to, if they do not wish to.

Small motor skills are developed more finely now, and children in first and second grade will enjoy activities that let them use these skills. Many children this age will enjoy doing puzzles, mazes, and more detailed art or activities, and the finished results will usually give them great pleasure.

First and second graders are eager to learn about the world and about God and Jesus. As they begin to be better readers, they will also enjoy reading things in their own Bibles, although the skills to find certain verses and passages in the Bible are still a little too difficult for them to master.

Even though they are eager to learn more from and about God's Word, children in this age range are still too young for detailed theological explanations. First and second graders are now able to begin to differentiate between and understand certain terms and concepts within Bible stories and see how these relate to their own lives.

Third and fourth graders

Third and fourth graders—the "middlers" in elementary school-age children—enjoy church school, not so much for the academic portion (they have gotten enough of that in the school room) but for the chance to see friends and to build those relationships. This is a prime age for encouraging friendships within the group that will sustain them throughout the turbulent adolescent years to come.

Children in this age group have begun to develop their leadership and organizational skills and will enjoy working within smaller groups on projects and learning activities. Because most of them can read fairly well, they will be able to follow written directions and may become very absorbed in certain projects. Research activities using a concordance, a Bible, and other religious resource books, will be a fun way for the students to integrate what they know academically with the religious curriculum. It is good to note, however, that most children in third and fourth grade prefer to involve themselves in active rather than reflective kinds of activities.

Just as with younger children, it is good to have a predictable routine or schedule within the classroom. Be sure to incorporate some quiet time within the schedule, but remember that with the longer attention span of this group of children, you can have learning activities that take twenty minutes or more, including projects that are continued from one week to the next.

Because children at this age seek to belong, it is important to their faith development that the teacher and other students accept them for who they are. Your positive reactions and acceptance will lead the way for the other students in the class.

Third and fourth graders are quite capable of using their Bibles. Because of their growing language skills, including dictionary skills and use of library materials, with proper direction they will become quite proficient at locating verses and passages in their Bibles. You can also encourage them to be responsible for remembering to bring their Bibles or other materials to class each time that you meet, as well as making them responsible for memorizing certain prayers or Bible verses.

Fifth and sixth graders

Fifth and sixth graders are enthusiastic, capable students. They have most of the basic skills necessary to really begin to study and learn from their Bibles and other materials, but they still need time to do some of the "activity" things that make learning fun.

Most fifth and sixth graders can read well, but that does not mean that they can read well aloud. Be cautious with the amount of time you ask fifth and sixth graders to read aloud, choosing other alternatives such as partner reading. Because of their beginning questions about "Who am I?" and "Where do I fit in?" it is important for the teacher to make the classroom setting as comfortable as possible.

Fifth and sixth graders are good at asking questions. They will want to know how and why, most often in reference to the question, "How does this relate to my life?" Especially when teaching Bible stories or values, the teacher needs to make the information relevant to the lives and experiences of the students.

These students have a highly developed sense of fairness and they can be judgmental or hard on others. They are beginning to experiment with developing their own opinions, but because they have such a sense and need to belong, some fifth and sixth graders will be overly cautious about expressing their opinions and views about important topics. Foster a sense of self-worth and respect for each child in the class, and your lead will encourage the children to react in the same way.

Fifth and sixth graders need to feel that they belong to the worshiping community as well, so incorporate into your class time some of the worship prayers, hymns, or litanies used by your church. Then when these students are in the worship service, they will be able to join in with the entire congregation.

Junior high

Adolescence is a time of major changes. Not only are the bodies of these youth changing physically and uncontrollably, but twelve- to fourteen-year-olds are experiencing emotional and intellectual changes as well. In addition, abstract thinking skills are emerging more strongly and students are beginning to discover new ways to approach the things that they have known.

It is still important to have a predictable class routine; more so that the students understand the level of expectation you have for them, than for security or comfort. You will also need to be flexible.

This age of students has a high need for acceptance by the peer group, so even though they may have definite opinions and views about certain subjects, they will not always be eager to discuss their opinions until they know what others in the group feel or think.

Junior high students have a greater ability to discuss, explore, research, and grasp information than younger age groups. Their reasoning skills will cause them to question what part God and the Bible play in their lives, but they can grasp some of the abstract concepts such as the Trinity or God as three in one. Encourage their questions as part of the acceptance they need and help them find answers.

As you spend time with the youth, your interest in them and your care and concern for them will encourage each one to become the person God wants him or her to be. Challenge them to make time for a prayer and devotional life outside of the classroom. Most importantly, know that these students look to teachers and other adults as role models, and the way that you express your own faith and belief will be a positive witness to them.

Faith development in children

"Now faith is being sure of what we hope for and certain of what we do not see" (Hebrews 11:1). The faith journey of each individual is a personal, unique experience. In recent years, interest has increased regarding the stages of faith development, especially within the context of Christian education. As teachers, we want to be able to nurture and guide the students we teach in their faith development. And we want to help the students we teach to find where God fits into their lives today. Even though the development of faith is a personal journey, we as a community of believers are to support, nurture, and challenge one another in our growing faith.

Some teachers have told me that they learn more about their faith from the children they teach than the children learn from them! An important part of the teaching process is to help the teacher to continue his or her own faith development as well.

Faith can be difficult to define. In fact, when we think we have come up with a definition, an added twist or thought from another person's point of view will challenge our definition and cause us to begin the process all over again.

In order to get us started, let's begin by using this definition of *faith*: "Faith is not simply knowledge or an understanding of who God is and what God does. Faith is an action we partake in as a response to the God who is an integral part of our lives."

What are some characteristics of a life of faith?

- We have trust and security in God and God's Word.
- We accept God's loving forgiveness.
- We identify ourselves as followers of Jesus Christ.
- We believe that God is active in our lives and in the world today.
- We acknowledge a commitment to loving service of others as a way of sharing God's love.
- We share the hope and assurance that there is a resurrection and eternal life.
- We lead a life of prayerful communication with God.

These characteristics of faith are reflected in a child's physical and intellectual growth. They cannot be separated. To nurture a child's faith, you must also consider the needs of his or her mind and body, and vice versa.

Consider these ways to nurture one another's faith in God.

- Participate in the life of the church and in regular worship.
- Study and reflect on God's Word, and share your thoughts with others.
- Spend regular time in prayer and reflection of God's will and God's way.
- Be aware of and sensitive to the actions of God in all of life, not just in your own life.
- Act in love and service toward all of God's creation in response to God's love for you.
- Share stories with others, both from the Bible and from your own life.
- Apply Bible truths in your everyday words and actions.

Stages of faith

You are probably aware of the many books and charts that help monitor a child's development, physically and mentally. You may not know that similar books and charts explain and explore faith development.

Although measuring faith development is less tangible than height or weight, faith does change and mature in some predictable ways. James Fowler has categorized certain faith characteristics into six stages of faith development. Three of the stages are summarized here. These stages are not a rigid process. Note that each stage suggests an approximate age, but not all people's faith develops at the same rate. Some students may seem to be "ahead" or "behind" according to these stages. That is not as important as recognizing that as a teacher, you can present information in different ways to help different students. For a more detailed exploration of this topic, see Life Maps: Conversations on the Journey of Faith by James W. Fowler and Sam Keen, Word, 1978.

Stage 1: God is like mom or dad

(approximate age range: two to six years old)

Children rely on those who love, care for, and nurture them. Their trust is transferred to God as a caring, loving parent who protects and nurtures them.

A teacher can nurture faith development at this stage in the following ways:

- Tell simple stories with a single focus. Remember that these children are literal learners.
- Avoid abstract ideas that might be misunderstood and will need to be unlearned later.
- Avoid overteaching. Be sure students understand the meaning of the words before taking them to another level of understanding.

- *Take advantage of students' willingness to join in spontaneous prayer or worshipful singing.*
- *Be truthful. Say, "I don't know" when you don't. The trust these children have for you will transfer to trust in God. You are the example of the love and acceptance God has for them.*

Stage 2: What's fair is fair

(approximate age range: seven to twelve years old)

Children in this stage begin to develop a definite sense of fairness. They are attracted by simple stories, but they still have a literal understanding of them. They can oftentimes only see good or evil—justness or fairness—in the stories. At this stage, the children often express their faith as "good people receiving blessings" or "bad people being punished."

A teacher can nurture faith development at this stage in the following ways:

- *Tell stories that present a positive image of God and God's actions. Concepts like forgiveness, stewardship, and concern for others need to be presented carefully. Stories need to have clear messages as to how they relate to the children's lives today.*
- *Discuss ways that people reflect their faith in action. These children are extremely interested in the kinds of things that people do to live out their faith. Invite someone to visit your class who has done missionary work or who works for an organization that helps others.*
- *Involve the children with other people in the congregation. They need to know that they belong and that they can contribute something of value to the community of faith.*
- *Provide opportunities for prayer, worship, and praise within the classroom setting and encourage private Bible reading and devotions. Whenever possible, incorporate portions of your worship service or liturgy into class time. This will give the children confidence to participate more fully when they are part of the worshiping community.*

Stage 3: I believe what the church believes

(approximate age range: beginning at about twelve years old)

People in this stage rely on authorities or leaders to define what they believe. They rarely spend time in a critical reflection of what they believe or why they believe as they do. Because of their broader social contacts, people in this stage are exposed to conflicting authorities, but their beliefs and understanding of God are drawn exclusively from what the church teaches.

A teacher can nurture faith development at this stage in the following ways:

- *Encourage the students' developing ability to ask questions and engage in discussions. You can also provide more complex ideas to fit their expanding world and viewpoints.*
- *Recognize the growing understanding of God as a personal friend, comforter, and advisor. Encourage their prayer and devotional life, and express your own faith in God and the role that God's plays in your life. Make them aware of the faith witness of other Christians as well.*
- *Help these students feel good about what they know and encourage them to use their intellectual knowledge to help them begin to develop their own opinions.*
- *Affirm each person as an individual, created in God's image and loved by God.*
- *Encourage and utilize activities that will help build relationships. Group projects, research assignments, or partner work will help foster relationships within the classroom.*

"For this very reason, make every effort to add to your faith . . ." (2 Peter 1:3-7). This passage from 2 Peter continues by listing the qualities and characteristics that Christians seek to have as part of their lives: goodness, knowledge, self-control, perseverance, godliness, kindness, and love. Through these qualities we can have a fruitful and abundant life that is pleasing to God and helpful to others. These qualities will help teachers to share God's love with their students. These very qualities will help us to achieve the excellence that we strive for in Christian education, be it in a weekly Bible study, in vacation Bible school, or in Sunday school.

This pursuit of excellence in any Christian education program causes exciting things to happen. The hour each week that is set aside for Christian education is more than just an hour between services, or a place to take the kids, or a time to share coffee and donuts. It is a time for exploring, guiding, and nurturing the growing faith of the children we teach and our own faith as well.

Many variables affect what takes place in a classroom. As you prepare to teach, you need to be aware of both the internal and external factors involved in creating a climate for learning. This chapter will explore some ways to enhance your teaching through things you do within and outside the classroom.

The classroom or space in which you and your students meet is your *learning environment.* Some churches are fortunate to have more than adequate space for meeting with a variety of groups while others cope with crowded conditions. Whatever your situation, your class area should be one where learning together is a pleasant and exciting experience. Above all, your classroom or meeting place should be a child-centered space.

The following suggestions and ideas will help you to make the most of the space you have. Try a variety of these suggestions and consider changing them periodically to maintain your students' interest. Whenever possible, involve your students in the decorating and maintenance of the classroom; it will give them real ownership and a feeling of belonging.

Climate indicators

When we use the word *climate,* we are usually referring to the weather or to the temperature. In the learning environment, we can use the word *climate* to gauge how a place or a situation feels to the people who are there. What is the climate in your classroom? Does the room invite people to enter? Is the atmosphere welcoming? Do the room arrangement, displays, and activities intrigue the students enough that they want to come in and become a part of the class?

The following questions about the climate of your learning environment can help you make sure that your classroom is one that welcomes and invites participation.

- *Are guests, visitors, or first-time students made to feel welcome?* You can put visitors at ease with simple gestures: show them where to hang their coats, offer to share a book with them, or invite them to sit down next to you. Be an example for your students and show them how to welcome and greet others. Talk about hospitality early on in the year so that the children are prepared for times when guests or visitors may be in class.

- *Are students and teachers accepted for who they are?* Is everyone made to feel that he or she belongs to the family of God and that each individual is unique because of who he or she is? Of all of the places that children gather in groups, the church classroom needs to be a place where everyone is treated with love and respect. All children need to know that they are included within the class activities, just as they are included within the family of God. Again, as you model love, acceptance, and forgiveness to all students, the students themselves will reflect the same attitudes.

- *Are people encouraged to communicate their thoughts, feelings, and ideas in the classroom?* Do they feel that, even though everyone may not always agree with them, they are respected for their individualism? Being a part of a Christian community means being willing to listen to and talk with one another. When people share their thoughts and feelings within the context of a Christian setting, their faith can be nurtured and stretched. As people realize that they are respected and appreciated for their opinions, they will be able to better listen to and care for others.

- *What part does the Sunday school or Christian education program play within your congregation?* A strong education program needs the support of the entire congregation. Some ways to foster a good relationship with the Sunday school and congregation include regular programs to which the entire congregation is invited, inviting members of the congregation into the classroom as guest lecturers, involving classes in portions of the worship service, including teachers and classes in the prayers of the church, posting a schedule of upcoming Sunday school or vacation Bible school events, and noting Sunday school activities or achievements in the church's bulletin or newsletter.

Arranging your classroom

The ideal classroom is a bright, roomy space with plenty of natural light, soft neutral paint on the walls, some area of the floor carpeted, some tiled. It contains age-appropriate furniture, has adequate storage space, and is well-insulated against disruptive outside noise. The actual classroom, on the other hand, may exhibit some of these features, but probably not all. As a teacher, you will need to work with the space you have been given. Following are some ideas for how to create a warm, pleasant, child-centered environment, using the space available to you.

Room arrangement

If possible, create a number of learning areas within your classroom by rearranging furnishings to match your activity. If you have the luxury of a large space, you might set up separate learning areas permanently.

Use carpet squares, large floor pillows, bean bag chairs, or an area rug to establish a place for storytelling. Do projects at a work table. Display items on window sills, shelves, or a table. Decorate bulletin boards or free-standing display centers with posters, teaching pictures, and students' artwork. Make your classroom as welcoming as possible!

Whenever possible, it is better to have moveable chairs and tables in a classroom so that you can be flexible in the way you arrange them each time that you meet. Individual desks and chairs or chairs with a hinged desk that folds down seem to work better with older students or adults than with little children.

When using tables and chairs or benches with younger children, make sure that the chairs are child-size and that the tables are adjusted to fit the children's height when sitting on the chairs. Simple benches could be set up in a corner as a reading or storytelling area by painting several boards and setting them on top of cinder blocks or a wooden base at the children's height.

Fun furniture

Involve parent volunteers in making some fun furniture for your classroom. A giant caterpillar, or other segmented animal, can be made with large pillows. The pillows can be separated for sitting on, then stuck back together again when cleanup time arrives.

To make a caterpillar, cut a round or oval pillow pattern approximately 3 feet in diameter. Use large pieces of fabric or sheets and cut two sections for each segment of the caterpillar. Pin the sections, right sides together, then stitch around them. Leave an opening of about 6". Then stuff and sew up the opening. Add a strip of Velcro brand fastener or snaps along both sides of each pillow section, being sure that each section has the same number of snaps so that the pillows will fasten together easily. Fasten the caterpillar sections together, forming the body.

Select one pillow to be the head. Add feelers and facial features from felt or other fabric as shown. The finished caterpillar will sit against one wall when not in use, but will also break down to make individual seating when needed.

Classroom arrangement of desks, tables, or chairs will vary depending upon your teaching style, as well as the configuration of the room in which you are meeting. Some common classroom

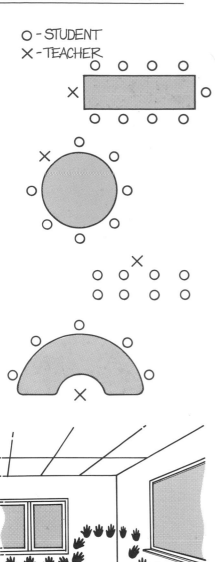

O – STUDENT
X – TEACHER

diagrams using a table and chairs or desks are shown here. Find a seating arrangement that works well for you and for your class, either one of those pictured here or another of your own choosing. (Chapter 5 focuses on teaching and learning styles and includes ideas for learning centers and classroom configurations.)

Color

Soft, neutral colors are best in a classroom. Not only will a fresh coat of paint brighten up a dark dingy room, but it will make it easier to add the children's artwork as part of the room decor. If your room needs to be repainted, you might suggest to the church's building committee that there be a "paint party," and enlist the help of parents and children to repaint the room.

A personal touch

How about personalizing the room you and the children will share by painting a handprint border all around the room? By using acrylic paints (the kind used for stenciling on walls and other materials) you can add a colorful, meaningful border that will serve as a type of growth chart for the children of your congregation.

To do this, pour a small amount of acrylic paint into a flat plate or tray. Then have the children practice pressing their hands into the paint and then printing their handprint on a sheet of paper before they print on the wall.

Use a yardstick to help you mark a pencil line around the room that the children will use as a guide. Help them press their hands into the paint and then onto the line on the wall. After they wash their hands, have them print their name, age, and the date underneath the handprints with a brush or permanent marker.

Acrylic paints will clean up easily with water, are non-toxic, and will dry in approximately twenty minutes. They are readily available in craft or fabric stores.

Storage

Storage space seems to be at a premium in most Sunday school classrooms. Whatever system your church uses for storing supplies and curriculum, it is important that a teacher has some of these materials available at his or her fingertips each class time.

A set of low bookshelves makes a nice place to store materials. Organize your supplies in a variety of labeled containers and set them on shelves. Some teachers use plastic dishpans for blocks, puzzles, and other toys and items used by young children in the classroom. Using dishpans, baskets, or well-marked boxes makes it easier for the children to clean up for themselves when they are done playing with an item.

You can create your own containers for storage in the classroom. Boxes of any size can be painted or covered with fabric or self-adhesive paper. You can also cover cans with paint, self-adhesive paper, or fabric. Egg cartons make good containers for small items such as buttons or rocks.

After covering any of these containers, you can glue an example of the item to the outside for easy identification, or glue a picture of the item to the box or can and print its name, using felt-tip pen.

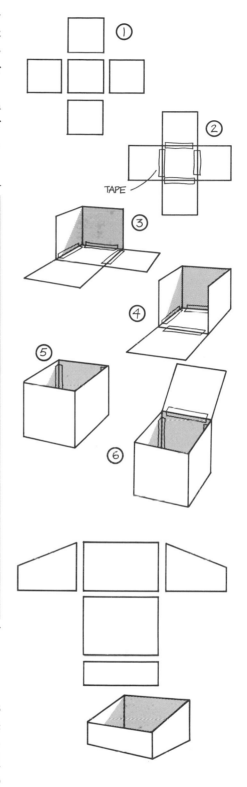

Boxes, boxes, boxes!

If you can't find a box in the exact size or shape that you need, design a custom-made box from cardboard or poster board. The materials you will need are: cardboard or poster board; masking tape; a ruler and a pencil; a utility knife or paper cutter that will cut cardboard; paint, fabric, or self-adhesive paper to cover the box when you are done.

To make a 12" cube, cut six 12" squares from cardboard or poster board. Place one square in the center and arrange the other four squares around it.

Tape each side to the center square. Then lift up two adjacent sides and tape them together at the corner. Lift up the other two sides and tape them together at the corner.

Tape the two corners that aren't yet taped. If you want a flat lid that opens, tape the last square to the top as shown:

Cover the box with paint, fabric, or self-adhesive paper if you wish.

These directions can be adapted for any size or shape that you like. For a file box, adjust your design so that the front and back sections are the same width but different heights (slope the back so that it is higher than the front). The base will be the same width as both front and back sections and the same length as the side sections. Cover the completed box if you wish.

Display space

Displaying artwork, especially the children's own artwork, makes the classroom an inviting place and helps to reinforce what the children are learning. There are many ways to display art, completed projects, posters, maps, and charts in a classroom. Several easy and inexpensive display suggestions are given here. Keep in mind that whatever you display on a wall should be at the eye-level of the students using the room.

Bulletin boards

Bulletin boards can be used in many ways in the classroom. Numerous books have instructions about planning and designing bulletin boards as well as actual patterns for bulletin boards. You may want to check for some of these books in your church library or at a local bookstore.

Involve students in creating and maintaining bulletin boards. If they are actively involved in creating a bulletin board display, they will be more interested in looking at it!

Also consider using the bulletin board as a review tool or as a further step in a particular learning. A bulletin board should catch your attention and cause you to think. This is not to say that a bulletin board should never be "just" for decoration, but whenever possible, try to make an attractive bulletin board with a message.

If you plan a year's worth of bulletin boards at once, you can coordinate the background paper and fasten it to the board at one time. Cut pieces of butcher paper or other background paper to fit the bulletin board, then staple each layer to the board, finishing with the color you will use at the beginning of the year. Then whenever you want to update or change the board, you can simply remove the top layer and you're ready to add the remainder of the display. You will save yourself a lot of the most time-consuming work if you do this all at one time.

Whenever possible, add a third-dimension to your bulletin board design. Accordion-pleated paper, rolled paper, yarn, string, fabric, and corrugated cardboard pieces will all add texture and dimension to your design. Adding a border makes a nice addition to the board as well. You can purchase some types of borders and lettering in education or teacher supply stores, but it is also easy to make your own, either freehand or with patterns.

Use lettering to add a title, thought-provoking question, or direction to the completed bulletin board. Be sure to title any student's work that is on the bulletin board, adding their name, age, and comments if applicable.

Although most Sunday school classrooms have wall-mounted bulletin boards, you may be using a room that is used by other groups during the week or one where you cannot leave your bulletin board or display in place. Some of the following alternative ideas may work for you.

Other wall display ideas

If you do not have wall-mounted bulletin boards in your classroom, it might be possible to mount a type of cork strip on your walls. These strips are edged with metal, mount with screws and can be cut to any length you wish. Decide how high to mount the strips according to the eye level of the children who will be using the room.

If your walls are cloth-covered, it is difficult to tape or even pin display items to them. One solution is to purchase a roll of self-adhesive Velcro brand fastener and use small pieces of the

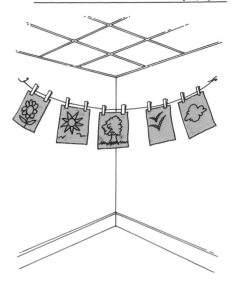

"looped" side. Fasten these pieces to the corners of your poster or artwork and they should stick securely to the wall.

A kiosk made from a free-standing bulletin board or even from graduated boxes stacked on top of one another as shown can also make a nice alternative to a bulletin board or display space. In some cases, the boxes will even stack one inside the other for easy storage between classes.

A clothesline hung in the room makes a good display place for children's artwork. Eye hooks can be fastened in two corners of the room and a line strung between them, or you can even arrange the hooks so that the line is strung across the corner. Art can be clipped to the line with clothespins or paper clips, and this will also make a nice place to hang painted pieces as they dry.

Unclaimed space

How about using the classroom door as a display space? Some Sunday schools use this unclaimed space for a display that reflects the students who are a part of the class or another message that they want others to see. You can cover the door with butcher paper or other background paper and decorate as you wish.

The hallway is another often overlooked place where you and your students can share your work or projects with other people in your congregation. One example I have seen is a border of footprints leading to a classroom door. The students had printed their names on the footprints and added the words "We are following Jesus . . . Come join us!" What a fun way to identify the children in the class and share a message about what they were doing and learning!

Mobiles make wonderful displays, use space that no one else is usually using, and almost anything can be hung from the ceiling. Use ceiling pipes, light fixtures or even acoustic ceiling tile as a base for hanging items that the students have made and want to display in the classroom. The arrangement of some ceiling tiles makes it especially easy to hang art or mobiles from them. Attach a piece of string to the art, and tie a large paper clip to the other end. Slip the paper clip under the metal strip that the ceiling tiles rest on and you will have a free-hanging display space.

Enrich the environment

Your classroom environment can be enriched in many ways. The goal is not to add so many distractions that the students are disrupted in the learning process, but to enhance the learning that takes place through visual and manipulative items.

Books on shelves and pillows to sit on are inviting and will offer alternatives for students who arrive early or end up waiting a few minutes for a parent at the close of class.

Assorted scrap materials such as paper, cloth, paper tubes, ribbons, and other items usually considered "junk" are great finds for children who have a need to create.

Plants add life and color, offer the opportunity to think about responsibility when it comes time to water them, and can be a good lesson in the beauty of the world that God has created.

Small animals such as hamsters, gerbils, or even a few goldfish in a bowl can be brought to class to offer children the chance to observe part of God's creation.

Baskets of blocks or other manipulative items can involve the children in creating or building, but can also be a good lesson in sharing with others.

Use your own judgment when planning or adding enrichment items to your classroom so that the items you add will not disrupt you or the learning environment you are striving to create.

Making contact with students

It is important to keep in touch with your students both inside and outside the classroom. If you are up on what is happening in their lives, you will be better equipped to positively nurture their faith development. Here are a few ideas to help you keep up with your students.

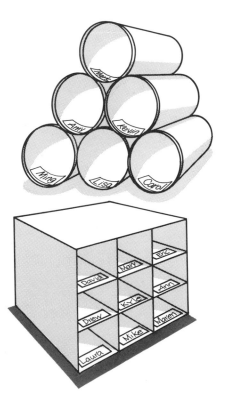

- Set up a mailbox system in your classroom where you leave personal notes or messages for your students. Some cardboard beverage cartons are already divided into slots that can be labeled for the students. Or you can attach separate shoe boxes together to make your own system. Cans or other round containers can also be fastened together and labeled for each individual student.

  One of the nice things about having a mailbox system is that the students can put away their completed work in their own slots until class time is over.

  Students will look forward to receiving a personal note or letter from you each time they come to class and they can be encouraged to leave notes or messages for each other in the mailboxes as well.

- A class newsletter is a fun project that the students can contribute to as well as enjoy receiving. Include Bible verses, puzzles, things to do at home, and other messages from you in the newsletter. You could put together a newsletter once a month and either mail it or put it in the students' individual mailboxes.

- Create a monthly class calendar that includes a Bible reading for the day as well as an inspirational thought or something fun to do.

- A phone call or letter before a special event, at the beginning of a term, or when a student has been absent will be appreciated and will let the student know that you enjoy and appreciate having him or her in class. Some Sunday schools send postcards to students who have been absent for one or more times. If your Sunday school does not have this policy, you might want to suggest that they try it.

- Most school systems have "conferences" where they meet either with students, or parents, or both. Why not try informal "conferences" during class time as a way to get better acquainted with the children who are in your class? Scheduling a few minutes of time with each child will really pay off! Not only will you both get to know a little bit more about each other, you will be showing them by your actions that you value them for who they are. It has been said that the most valuable gift we can give children is our time, and children know and appreciate when someone spends a few minutes with them just for fun.

Involving families

Although you will come to know your students during class time, you may or may not know the families of the children in your class. Make a point to let your students' parents and family members know that they are partners with you in the education of their children. Keep in touch with families by incorporating some of these ideas:

- Some curriculum has a note to the family included as a part of each session. If the curriculum you are using does not, you might print up a short note for the children to take home each week that tells some of the things you have been doing together in class and what kinds of things families might do together at home to extend or reinforce the learning. This is also a good way to let families know of special programs coming up or the need for volunteer help or supplies in the coming weeks.

- Plan a family lesson or an open house. You might suggest to the director of your Sunday school that your entire Sunday school plan an open house together. Or you could plan an open house as a combined effort between several classes. Include a short program with the children sharing some of the things they have been learning such as songs, a play, or memory work. Hang their artwork or completed projects in the room and provide simple refreshments for the guests.

- Occasionally, send home "I caught your child doing something good" notes. Don't make it a point to only contact parents or family members when there is a conflict or problem to be resolved. Let parents know when their children have been kind to another person, when they have grasped a biblical truth in a new way, or when they have been exceptionally helpful.

Involving the congregation

Sometimes the Sunday school seems to be a separate entity within a church. Any of the following suggestions can be good starting points to keep members of the congregation aware of what children in the church are doing.

- Include a page in your church's monthly newsletter that details the things you have been studying or doing in Sunday school. All of the classes may want to contribute to this page. Include the Bible stories you have been reading, art projects you have completed, or service projects that you are involved in. You might also tell the congregation where the Sunday school offering is going.
- Check with the person who is responsible at your church for bulletin covers used for Sunday worship services. Perhaps some of your students' original artwork could be photocopied and used for a special service.
- Designate a bulletin board or display in the church building where Sunday school classes can show what kinds of things they have been doing in class.
- Ask the pastor or worship planning committee to include you and your class in the prayers of the church during the worship service. How about setting up a rotating schedule that will make sure that all teachers and students are included in the prayers on a regular basis?
- Check for ways that your class and other classes can be a part of the worship service. Perhaps you have written a class prayer or litany that you could share with the congregation, or some students would like to read the scripture lessons on a Sunday morning for the service. Maybe your class could volunteer as ushers for a service or could stay after the service to help straighten up. By making sure your students play a visible part in your church, you not only let adult members know that the children are part of the church, but you give the students an opportunity to be involved in the community of believers in a relevant and meaningful way. They will take great pride in what they can do for others in the church.

No magic formulas can guarantee a well-run classroom—one that encourages positive behavior or that is a comfortable, organized place to learn. But there are "tricks of the trade" that educators use to help them maintain the type of classroom that runs effectively and efficiently for them. Some of these tricks are learned by trial and error, but others can be passed along by colleagues.

The way that I manage my classroom is most likely different from the way you manage yours or the teacher down the hall manages his. Yet the thoughts and suggestions given here are basic, tried-and-true ideas that, when adapted to fit the unique needs of both you and your students, can help your classroom to be one that is manageable and a joy in which to teach!

Success and responsibility

Successful classroom management begins with a plan. You cannot expect to have a smoothly run class without some preparation. This includes being well-prepared to teach the lesson, having all the supplies on hand, and planning carefully what activities will work best with your group.

I keep two words in mind as I plan for any group that I teach: *success* and *responsibility*. As a teacher, I believe that every student in my class has the need and the right to be successful. I want my students to have a good sense of self and to know that they are loved and accepted for who they are—children of God. Of all places, the Christian classroom is one where children should feel loved, accepted, and respected.

As I plan each class session, I make sure that I take into account a variety of things: objectives to be learned, experiences that will make the learning meaningful, the amount of time I have in which to teach, and, most importantly, how to make the session one where each child is able to be successful.

I do not mean just academic success. I am not just helping my students to be successful at memorizing the books of the New Testament or the Ten Commandments. The bottom line for me is that whatever is learned becomes a meaningful and significant part of each student's life, and that does not always mean the same thing for each child.

It is important for each teacher to define his or her idea of what constitutes success for each student, and to make sure to take every opportunity to get to know each child individually so that the level of learning, or the success level, is truly geared to who each child is, not to a preset list of objectives. This is especially important within the context of the Christian classroom because we cannot always measure or determine how faith grows.

The Christian classroom is also a wonderful place to begin to teach students the importance of responsibility. It is crucial that students are given the opportunity to make choices and decisions and then to be responsible for the choices they make.

Parents, struggling with this issue, often begin with small steps such as offering their children the choice of wearing a red shirt or a blue shirt, *not* the choice of wearing a shirt or not wearing a shirt. Teachers can begin by offering students smaller choices, such as, "Would you like to use crayons or markers to color this picture?"

When we provide students with opportunities to make responsible choices we are instilling skills and values that they will use for the rest of their lives.

Rules for keeping peace

Establishing rules for the classroom is not always an easy thing to do, but it is essential. It is best to tailor-fit your rules for order and safety to your class. What works for one class may not work for another.

Whenever possible, involve the students in deciding what rules you will have in the classroom. Even with young children, ask for their ideas about some good classroom rules, write them on a chalkboard, and discuss which ones everyone thinks are the most important.

From my own experience, I suggest you have only a few "don't" rules. Choose two or three things that you will not tolerate in the classroom, and then go from there. You may decide that your rules include "No talking out of turn" and "No running in the classroom during Sunday school." Another teacher may decide on different rules.

To balance the "don't" rules, always include "do" rules in your class, such as, "Always bring your Bible to class" or "Be sure to share with others."

One rule of thumb to keep in mind when determining classroom rules is anything that is unsafe or disruptive to the learning of another student should not be allowed. Because everyone in the class has a right to be safe and to learn, anything that might disrupt this becomes a "don't" rule. Other than those kinds of rules, try to maintain a more positive list of expectations for the students. And you might include a couple of silly rules, just for fun!

Attention getters and boredom beaters

There will be times when your students have just arrived in class and are chatting with one another, or when they are so involved in an activity that they will not notice you are trying to get their attention. Here are some attention getters that always seem to work!

- Turn off the lights in the classroom.
- Change the noise level or vary the volume of your voice. For instance, instead of raising your voice to speak above the class, start whispering. When a teacher does this, the children usually begin to talk more softly, too.
- Ring a bell or a timer.
- Play music.
- Use a puppet or a stuffed animal to "talk" to the students.
- Tell a joke or riddle.
- Begin a clapping pattern and get the students actively involved in echoing or repeating it after you.
- Write a message on the chalkboard with a direction to follow. For example, "Take out your Bible and find Chapter 5 in Matthew. When you have found it, fold your hands on your desk."
- Determine a signal that everyone copies, such as putting your hands on your head. When all of the students have also done this, you will be able to see that you have everyone's attention.
- Dramatize something for effect. For example, begin reciting your Bible memory verse in a Shakespearean accent or to a rap rhythm.

No matter how hard you try, or how well your lesson is planned, the time will come when the students in your class are bored. This doesn't necessarily reflect on you or on your teaching. It could very well be that some of the children didn't get enough sleep the night before, or that they have heard this particular Bible story every year for the past three years! In cases like these and others that you will run into, it helps to have a few "boredom beater" tricks up your sleeve! Plan your class time with these in mind, and add others that work for you.

- Evaluate the kinds of visuals you are using. If you always tell the Bible story with a flannelboard, try something else. Or involve the children more by having them place the figures on the flannelboard. Do you have access to a VCR and a video that presents the story in a different way? Consider all the visual options available to you.
- Take a risk and try an activity that you're not sure you will like doing; you might be surprised! If you always lean towards certain kinds of activities, the children may be pleased to try something new and different also.

- How can you involve all of the children in the story or activity? Sometimes students are bored when they see no reason to pay attention or listen. For example, when telling the story of the woman and her lost coin, embellish it by having the children "count" the coins aloud with you, always coming up one short until you reach the end of the story. Or perhaps have them draw pictures to illustrate the story as you tell it.

- When asking children to read portions of the story, it is easy to overlook the ones who have not volunteered to read. Try "partner reading" where each student reads aloud to a partner, then they switch and reread the same section or alternate paragraphs. In addition to involving everyone actively, this also frees you up to help any children who may need it, either with reading the passage or beginning the activity.

- Ham it up! Show the students another side of yourself that will keep their interest. Because children today are so used to being entertained, you might try to get their attention by dressing up as a Bible character and telling them your story. Stay in character and answer any questions they may have as well.

- One great example I saw of this was one teacher who retold the story of Mary and Martha. Using only a shawl, she was able to portray both women by moving the shawl from her shoulders to her head and slightly changing her voice at the same time. It was easy to determine who was who, and her presentation kept everyone on their toes, including her!

- Utilize resource people in your congregation and in your community. Guest speakers can always add a new and different dimension to your class time. If they are willing to answer questions or be a part of a follow-up discussion, they can stimulate the students' thinking beyond the classroom setting.

Nuts and bolts that hold it all together

- **Never smile until Christmas.** *Perhaps this is a bit overstated, but don't try so hard to be a friend to your students that they take advantage of classroom time and misbehave. Do smile in your class, and often, but be sure to have a definite idea of what limits you have for behavior, and what expectations you have for students.*

- **Ask veteran teachers for help and advice.** *Don't hesitate to ask experienced teachers for their advice, help, or suggestions. It can be both helpful and fun to have someone with whom you can discuss ideas or problems.*

- **Pay attention to the quiet students. The disruptive ones will always get the attention they are seeking.** *This may be easier said than done, but it is important to keep in mind. Quieter students need positive attention too. In addition, when the more disruptive students notice that other children get attention when using a quieter voice or by more subdued actions, they may follow suit!*

- **If you are tempted to say no to a request, stop and count to ten before you answer.** *It is oftentimes easier to say no than to give children the flexibility to try something that may not be in your lesson plan. But sometimes activities initiated by the students are the ones that make the greatest impact on their learning and their lives.*

- **Teach responsibility by giving students the opportunity to accept responsibility.** *This means allowing younger children to distribute papers or take the offering basket to the Sunday school office. With junior high students who are unhappy with the type of study you are doing, this may mean dividing the class into teams and letting each team plan a lesson. When students know that you respect and trust their ability to do something, they generally live up to your expectations.*

- **I can see you like red!** *Be conscious of the way your words can make a difference to a child's sense of self-worth. Try to make nonjudgmental comments that encourage the student to tell you more about his or her work or idea. Saying something like, "I can see that you really like red!" when looking at a picture of something you can't identify is better than asking, "What is it?"*

- **On the level.** *Whenever possible, speak to the children you are teaching at their level, bending down or kneeling, if necessary. Use language that means something to the children. Don't talk down to them, but define any words that you are not sure they understand. Remember, your students will live up (or down!) to your expectations of them, and sometimes using more sophisticated language (that you have defined for them) will make them feel more responsible for their words and actions.*

Discipline in the classroom

Each student comes to your classroom with an individual personality and his or her own set of already learned behaviors. Different combinations of students can result in totally new behaviors for certain students, and when these new experiences are coupled with a new teacher, different classroom rules, and new material to be learned, even children themselves may be surprised by the way they act and react.

The way that even the physical space and equipment is arranged can affect children in such a variety of ways that it is oftentimes hard to predict what is best for everyone involved.

Knowing that it is not any one thing that affects or determines a student's behavior is a good starting point for a teacher. Adding together all the factors—choice of curriculum and its age-appropriateness, special needs of learners, and time limits—will help to ensure that the behavior that takes place within your classroom is the best it can be.

"How should we discipline?" is one of the questions I am most often asked at workshops and teacher training events. It is a hard question to answer because there are many differing methods and viewpoints in regard to what discipline is, how to incorporate Christian love in discipline, and just what can be done to discipline students whom you may see for only 45 minutes a week.

Teaching children always involves discipline. In fact, the word *discipline* has some of the same roots as the word *disciple,* involving instruction and teaching. It is important to know that *discipline* does not necessarily mean "punishment." Jesus disciplined his followers and taught them to know, love, and respect God. We need to do the same with the children we teach.

One goal of educators is to instill a sense of self-discipline in the children we teach. Self-discipline is a necessary part of life—a skill that will help students to function as individuals but also as a part of society.

Discipline can be a positive way of solving conflicts, employing mutual respect for all parties involved. When discipline is done correctly, it shows lovingly what was done wrong, gives the child the responsibility for the problem, shows the child possible ways to solve the problem, and does not destroy the child's self-esteem.

Because children need to know where they stand, rules and routines offer them security. When one person upsets the security of another, it may be up to us as teachers to intervene. Consistent expectations and logical consequences will make behavior problems easier to handle in the church school setting.

To encourage a positive learning environment and maintain consistent behavior standards, you should consider the following:

- *Make the church school classroom a good place to be.* First of all, love and accept all the children in your class. Strive to reflect the unconditional love that God has for all people. Make sure that activities are meaningful and that there are many choices available to meet the individual needs of each child. Whenever possible, focus your attention on each child's positive behavior.

- *Be organized.* Be in tune to the children's needs when arranging the physical space in the classroom. Make sure that items you want them to see are at *their* eye level, not yours. Have your lesson plans intact when you arrive before class begins. Arrive early enough to set up the classroom if you were not the last person to use it. Maintain a regular routine, if possible, perhaps even printing your schedule on chart paper or a chalkboard so that the children know what to expect. For younger children, you might want to draw pictures to show what your schedule for the day is. For example, you could draw music notes for singing time and a cup and cracker to represent snack time.

- *Be flexible.* Even if you have made careful lesson plans, you need to remain open to the possibility of changing them. There *is* such a thing as the "teachable moment" especially when teaching in a Christian context. If it begins to snow during class time, you will be hard-pressed to keep the children's attention on the study of the Lord's Prayer. It is better to set that lesson aside, go to the window, and talk about the wonder and beauty of God's creation. You can be sure that this is a teachable moment and that the children will remember that each snowflake made by God is unique and different, just as they are. What a wonderful time to work on building self-worth and self-image!

  Be creative, too, with your room arrangement and schedule. For example, if your children come to you after sitting through a worship service, it doesn't make sense to sit them down again for a twenty-minute Bible story. Instead, reverse your natural inclination of order for the lesson and keep the children's interest as well.

- *Be firm, fair, and consistent.* Let the students know what your expectations are for them. Take time to go over classroom rules and acceptable behavior. You will not be wasting time to model for them and then spend class time practicing how to line up to go to music or how to collect papers in the class. Remember that you are their role model and they will imitate the way that you treat them. Your reactions will definitely determine the reactions of the rest of the class.

- *Give clear, concise directions.* Use a positive tone of voice when giving directions and remember that each direction can be broken down into many smaller parts, some of which may have to be learned. A simple rule of thumb is to not give more than three directions at one time. If more than one of the directions is a new behavior, give it alone or pair it with a well-learned direction. Delay giving new activity directions until the current activity is completed. Be aware of some of the unique needs of the students in your class and offer individual directions, if necessary, so that they will be able to follow the directions successfully. For example, one four-year-old that I was teaching had a hearing loss in his right ear. I made it a point to stand next to him, on his left side, whenever I gave the class directions. Then, after the children would begin working, I checked with him to be sure that he understood the directions.

It may be helpful for some classes to give both written and oral directions, or in the case of young children, visual and oral directions. It is a good idea to model the steps to the directions you are giving, as well as to check for the students' understanding of the directions. Some teachers pair children together and have them check with each other to make sure they understand the directions given.

- *Give students choices and reasons whenever possible.* Again, the expectations you have for the students in your class will be self-fulfilling. Let them know that you think they are responsible, capable people who can make good choices and decisions based on what they know and who they are. Help them to understand that when they are a part of a group, they have a responsibility to that group.

- *Set limits that everyone can live with.* Read through the information on page 32 that gives guidelines for determining classroom rules. When you have decided on which rules you as the teacher absolutely have to have, be sure to explain these to the students. Have them repeat to you the rules or explain them in their own words so that you are sure everyone understands what you expect. It wouldn't hurt to post the rules somewhere in the classroom as well, especially for times when you may not be able to be in class and a substitute is needed.

- *Encourage the children's questions and willingness to share their thoughts.* Be sure that you reflect an open, listening attitude. Share your ideas as well. Don't be afraid to say "I don't know" if you are not sure of the answer. Your students will respect your honesty.

- *Be interesting.* Make your lessons thought-provoking and fun! Challenge yourself to try new and different things in class. Incorporate a variety of learning and teaching techniques so that you reach the majority of the students. Keep them guessing as to what you're going to do next!

Causes of behavior problems

In the student

- Does the student have difficulty reading with his or her age group?
- Has the student been unsuccessful in previous school settings?
- Is the problem related to something happening in the family?
- Is the student using misbehavior as an attention-getter because of a lack of positive attention in other areas of his or her life?
- Could the misbehavior be related to poor listening skills, lack of study skills, or lack of interest in the material to be learned?

In the classroom atmosphere

- Is there lack of classroom organization?
- How much opportunity is there for student interaction or responsibility?
- Does the student have a part in planning and setting goals?
- Are directions, goals, and assignments clear? For example, is it difficult for the student to hear you? Does the student understand the assignments? Was the lesson discussed thoroughly?
- Are supplies and equipment easy to locate and use?

In the teacher's attitude

- Are you warm and friendly to all students?
- Are you consistent in expectations, rules, and requirements?
- Do you make fair and equal judgments when it is necessary to make a judgment?
- Are you even-tempered?
- Are you firm but fair?
- Do you have appropriate expectations for students at this age-level?

Correcting behavior problems

At some point it may be necessary to correct behavior problems taking place in the classroom. It is best to have given this some thought before you actually need to make the correction so that you will be prepared and can follow through in a consistent way.

The best way to correct any behavior problems within a church school setting is to guide the student into responsible self-control. In some cases, this may mean removing the student from the classroom or the situation until you can spend a private moment talking together about it.

It is important to remove the student for several reasons. When a short time has passed between the problem and the discussion about it, both the teacher and student will be more objective. Sometimes when a child is reprimanded in front of the class, he or she will look to the peer group for support and defense, perhaps even becoming a "hero," which benefits no one.

After separating the student so that you can deal with him or her individually, don't ask "why" questions such as "Why did you hit Pam with your pencil?" Asking "why" questions will only result in excuses and reasons. Instead, have the student tell you what he or she did. If this doesn't work, tell what you saw, but still refrain from asking why.

Once you have agreed on what the behavior was, make it clear to the student why that behavior is not acceptable and why it cannot be repeated.

Then redirect the student's activity into a more positive behavior. You may only need to suggest a more appropriate behavior or response to some children, while others will need to have you show them an appropriate behavior.

Some repeated misbehaviors require a logical consequence—one that ties directly to the behavior. One example of this is a "time out," used, for example, when a small group is playing a game and one child gets angry and upsets the gameboard. He or she may need to sit out the next game as a logical consequence of disrupting the other students' game.

It can be very helpful for the students themselves to determine the logical consequence that ties in with the inappropriate behavior. Together you can define the problem and explore different alternative consequences. After all options are discussed, involve the student in choosing the best alternative and then following through on it.

One of the greatest gifts that you can give to the children in your class is the knowledge that they are all unique children of God. Yet some of them will be extra special children who need your thoughtful planning and help throughout class time.

This chapter will present some thoughts about self-esteem and self-worth and will suggest ways to foster self-esteem in your students. In addition, ways to motivate students will be discussed, along with basic information to help teachers who are working with children who have special needs.

Fostering self-esteem

Because we are all made in God's image, we are valuable, loved people. Yet there will be children who, through no fault of their own, will not *feel* valued and may seem to be the most unlovable people you have ever met.

There are some basic messages that we as Christian educators must share with the children in our classes. The most important thing our students can learn is that God loves them enough to have sent Jesus to earth to be their Savior. To believe this is to be grounded in healthy self-esteem and wholesome self-worth. If they learn nothing else in your class but this, they will have learned enough.

God loves you

Following are six examples of faith messages that uphold a student's self-worth and help build self-esteem. See how many ways you can convey these messages through your teaching.
- *1. God loves you and so do I.*
- *2. God believes in you and so do I.*
- *3. God will be with you in every situation. God will help you and care for you.*
- *4. God listens to you and so will I.*
- *5. God cares for you and so do I.*
- *6. You are unique and important to God, and I think you are unique and important too.*

By just spending time with children, we let them know that they are important to us. But there are other ways that we let people know how important they are to us. Whenever we are building a relationship with someone, there are certain fundamentals that we depend on to help us. Although there is not always adequate one-on-one time with students when we are in a teaching situation, there are some ways to guarantee a good rapport with students.

Consider these things as the building blocks for a good relationship with your students.

- *Eye contact.* In North American culture, this is a fundamental part of working with anyone. Looking at students when talking with them can help to create a bond of closeness and improve communication.
- *Private time.* No matter how short, a private moment to speak with each student will make him or her feel that you truly value the relationship you are building.
- *Praise.* Everyone blooms when someone compliments or praises them. Look for opportunities to do this, especially with students who seem to lack self-confidence.
- *Involvement.* Whenever possible, involve the students in your class in small and large group projects and ask for their individual help or opinions as well. Asking for help is one of the quickest ways to involve a quiet learner, and your thanks after he or she has helped will make a world of difference. Everyone wants and needs to be acknowledged for their contributions, and everyone's contribution is significant, no matter how small.
- *Touch.* Research has shown how important physical touch can be to a person's development. Touch is an important part of nurturing relationships, and we usually feel the closest to the people we touch. We can often make a point stronger by putting a hand on someone's shoulders or by patting them on the back than by any amount of words that we may say.

  Be sure that your touch is appropriate and does not make your students uncomfortable. Depending on the age and sex of your students, it may be better to refrain from touching them.

Activities that build self-esteem

Building a student's sense of self-esteem and self-worth is something you can have a lot of fun doing! Try one or more of these suggestions in your classroom. Not only are they good builders of a student's self-esteem, but also a good way for students to get to know one another better.

Welcome, welcome!

Make sure that your classroom is a welcoming place when the students arrive. The way you set up your learning environment and your welcoming presence will go a long way in making children feel that you are glad they are a part of your class. Using each child's name and spending the time to make personal comments is a good start. Celebrating each student's birthday in a special way is another.

Kid of the day

Give each student a chance to be special for a day by designating a "kid of the day." Plan a special bulletin board that highlights accomplishments, interests, and a picture of the student. You can ask the parents to send in a picture of their child or take an instant photo yourself. Another nice addition to the bulletin board is to have all of the other students in class write or draw what they like best about the student to add to the display.

Peer profiles

Spend a few minutes brainstorming the kinds of questions people ask one another to find out more about them. You might want to write these questions on a chalkboard or a sheet of chart paper. Some questions might be, "What are your favorite hobbies?" "What is your favorite place to eat?" "Name someone that you admire."

Have the students draw a name of a classmate out of a hat or box and then interview that person, using the questions you have written or questions of their own. You might have them cut a silhouette of a person's head, write the information they discover on it, then post the silhouettes on a wall or bulletin board in the classroom. This activity can be extended one step further by having each student introduce to the rest of the class the person they have interviewed.

Handprints

Each person's handprint is a unique reminder of their individuality. Have the students make handprints by tracing their hands on a sheet of paper or by printing them on paper after dipping their hands into acrylic or tempera paint. Use the handprints in a mobile or as the border on a bulletin board. You might even make a border of handprints to go around your class door.

People scavenger hunt

A scavenger hunt is always fun, but especially when the "treasure" is getting to know someone better, or even getting acquainted with someone that you don't know at all.

In this activity, attributes that the students could discover in one another are listed on a chalkboard or a sheet of chart paper. For example, attributes such as *kind, patient, humorous,* and others could be listed.

Each student will need to search for and locate one member of the class who has at least one of these attributes, the goal being to find someone who fits each attribute. (Be sure to take part in this activity yourself!) Before you begin, be sure to explain these rules to your students.

- 1. No name may be used for more than two or three entries (depending on how many people are participating).
- 2. Students don't need to prove their acquisition of the attributes; their word will be taken.

Once students have written down the names of the people they have "discovered," call an end to the game and spend a little time discussing the "treasures" they found. Were there any surprises?

"Me" books

Let the students make books that tell something about themselves, and about their relationship to God. Use two pieces of construction paper for the cover and use brass fasteners or staples to hold the book together. Have the students decorate the front cover with a title such as "A book about . . ." and art of their choice.

Help them decide what to write and/or draw about themselves on each page. Following is a suggested table of contents.

- 1. This is me.
- 2. Here is my family.
- 3. This is my church.
- 4. This is my favorite color.
- 5. These are my friends.
- 6. This is something I like to do.
- 7. This is one way I like to help other people.

Other pages can be added if the children wish. For the sake of time, you may want to print up and duplicate the pages with the sentences already on them, perhaps with "dotted" letters for students who are beginning writers. When the books are completed, let the students read them aloud to the rest of the class, then take them home to share with their families.

Name prints

Everyone is proud of his or her own name and here is one way to make name prints that can be shared in the classroom or taken home.

These prints can be done with students who print or write their names. Each will make a somewhat different print.

Have the students fold a sheet of white construction paper in half the long way, then use tempera paint to print or write their names on one side of the folded paper, using the creased center as the bottom. The names must touch the fold line so that when the painting is done, the paper can be refolded and pressed together. This will make the name print both upside down and backwards on the other side of the paper. The finished design will look somewhat like a bug or mask design. Mount the prints on coordinating colors of construction paper and hang them in the classroom.

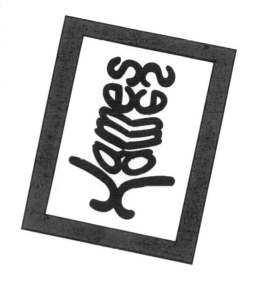

Motivation

Motivation is most certainly part of our behavior. In fact, motivation is often cited as the biggest problem in the business world. Some teachers assure me that it is the biggest problem in Christian education, too!

No matter what teaching skills you have, how well-prepared your lesson is, or what kind of exciting activities you include in your class time, a student's desire to learn is an essential ingredient in the teaching/learning process, and one over which you may think you have little control.

The relationship between the teacher and the student is an important factor in the area of motivation. Teachers who respect their students will make more of an impact on the students' desire to be a part of class. Students need to see that a teacher values their feelings and opinions, and they need to see that the teacher is someone who is learning along with them.

How can you have an impact on your students' motivation? Consider some of these ways.

- *Concern.* When students have a concern that relates to what is learned, they are wanting to see what a difference their knowledge makes. For example, students who have been exposed to facts and figures about hunger in the world will be more inclined to learn more, and especially to learn what they can do, when they discover someone they know has been hungry, or when they have traveled to a country where they have seen the effects of hunger.
- *Interest.* When a topic or subject is of particular interest to the students, it is easy to motivate them to research or learn more about the subject.
- *Goals.* Recognizing a goal motivates people, whether they are practicing to sing in a Christmas cantata or memorizing the Beatitudes for award Sunday. It helps to include the students in setting the goals because then they will have more invested in the goals they are trying to reach. They need to know where they are going and why. Another important factor of goal setting is the

association different goals have. For example, "I need to know or do this in order to be able to do that."

- *Success.* Success motivates. Students learn best when they feel successful and can see the results or consequences of what they have learned. Sometimes we can affect the motivation that success creates in the way that we say certain things. One example with a math study showed that when only mistakes were pointed out for correction, students responded with only a 20 percent gain or improvement. When the correct math problems were pointed out, however, there was a 70 percent improvement in the success rate of future math work.

- *Knowledge of results.* Everyone wants to know where they stand, especially in relationship to their improvement from previous work. It is harder to measure "results" in the field of religious education than in other more academic subjects, but the growth and nurture of faith is observable through both words and actions.

- *Intrinsic/extrinsic motivation.* Everyone has different ways that they react to intrinsic or extrinsic motivation. Although many teachers use stickers or other rewards in the classroom, their end goal is to help children learn to be successful (collecting a good number of stickers—the extrinsic reward) and then to realize that they enjoy learning so much that they don't even care if they get stickers anymore (intrinsic reward).

Any time that a teacher provides varied, pleasant learning experiences, most students will be motivated to pursue other learning experiences. When information is associated with a pleasant experience, it is remembered longer and there is motivation to continue in the learning process.

It is good to remember that variety is not only the spice of life, but a key ingredient to maintaining a student's interest and motivation!

Involving children who have special needs

Although all children are important, some of the children in your class may also have special needs. No matter what a child's special needs are, your attitude and reactions to that child will probably be the most powerful force in forming the attitudes and reactions of the other children in the class. Be prepared to help these children by doing some research and information-gathering as well as talking with their families, your pastor, or other professionals who can give you help in making the Christian education classroom a positive experience for everyone.

Consider the following factors as you prepare to teach:

- Remember, these children have as high a desire to be wanted and accepted as part of a group as other children do.
- Help build these children's sense of self-esteem by planning for group activities that they will be successful at.
- Be aware that at times, a special needs child may interrupt the flow of the session. (Some examples could include a distraction taking place in another part of the classroom or the lack of a student's developmental or manipulative skills necessary for the task at hand.)
- Students who have a physical disability may be limited physically, but not necessarily in other areas. These may be students who have great leadership skills or other strengths.

When you are aware of and plan to meet the needs of special needs students in your classroom you will not be doing anything different than what you would do to individualize and help any of the children in your classroom.

When planning to meet the needs of a learner with special needs, you should consider these strategies:

- *Get to know the student.* As with all students, one-on-one time is extremely important. Spend time getting to know personal information and stories about the students and telling them things about yourself as well. Don't focus on the disability but rather on each student's abilities. What you discover may help you in your session planning.
- *Talk to the family.* Parents and caregivers can give you valuable information that will help in teaching a particular child. No matter how much general information you have about a particular need, personal insights from the people closest to the student will be of the most benefit. Ask about teaching methods or styles that work well for the student and show family members that you care about the well-being of this person they love and care for.
- *Talk with professionals.* Check with your church school director for further advice from others who may have worked with this student or who are professionally trained in dealing with the student's particular needs.
- *Read books and current information about the specific needs of the student.* Check with your local library and the national organizations that have the most up-to-date information about working with children who have special needs. They will usually have creative ideas about how to integrate all children into the classroom and ensure that they have positive experiences.

Strategies for meeting special needs

"Special needs" is a broad term that relates to many different conditions. Here are some brief summaries and teaching helps for working with the most common special needs.

This information is intended to be just a starting point. Be sure to talk with parents and professionals who can offer you more help and suggestions as well. As you read about each particular special need, be aware that many of the suggestions pertain to all students, depending on the way that they learn best. (More information on "Learning Styles" can be found in Chapter 5. See pages 60–61.)

Students with learning disabilities

Students with learning disabilities often have average or even above average intelligence but do not achieve their potential. The teacher of a student who is learning disabled should consider these approaches:

- Establish realistic goals for and with the student.
- Have the student focus on the most essential information, rather than insisting that he or she cover all of the information.
- Provide options for information gathering, such as using a tape recorder, reading, or making something.
- Break assignments into smaller segments, perhaps even providing the younger student with picture clues that will help in completing the assignment.
- Note how long an attention span the student has and change the activity before he or she is too tired.
- Give the student a few specific questions to guide their reading.
- Check for understanding after directions are given to the entire group.
- Provide a class schedule for the student so that he or she can anticipate activities and shifts in activities.
- Note positive responses and actions the student uses to build up his or her self-esteem.

Students who are mentally retarded

A student who is mildly mentally retarded will benefit from being a part of a group with his or her peers. Those who have more retardation will not integrate as easily in a group of other students without more intentional effort. Teachers working with children who are mentally retarded should consider these approaches:

- Adapt curriculum to the reading and comprehension levels of the student.
- Use a variety of approaches whenever possible to reinforce a point. Take into account all of the possible learning styles and integrate them.
- Move from concrete experiences to those that are more abstract. For example, show an actual item, then a

photo, then a drawing, and then words that all represent the same thing. When using religious symbols and their meanings, this is very important.
- *Present materials to the student in small portions.*
- *Note the student's attention span and use several shorter teaching periods, rather than one of any great length, to cover the material.*
- *Whenever possible, have these learners experience what they are learning about (such as watching a Baptism).*
- *Add extra materials to the classroom for interest, particularly for students whose reading level is below other skills.*
- *Always help the student see how the learning and activities from class can be a part of his or her daily life as a Christian.*

Students with physical disabilities

Students with physical disabilities may need to use crutches, a cane, or a wheelchair to get from one place to another. They may also have health problems that are not visible, such as allergies, arthritis, or epilepsy.

Teachers who work with students who have observable physical disabilities should consider the following:
- *Locate the classroom in a place where easy movement of a wheelchair or crutches is possible so that the student is not physically frustrated when trying to get to class.*
- *Prepare places to store crutches or a walker when the student wants to be actively involved in a creative activity.*
- *See that tables are high enough for a wheelchair to fit under or provide a lapboard that is comfortable for the student.*
- *Let the student do as much for himself or herself as possible.*
- *Don't underestimate the student's mental capabilities or performance because of physical limitations.*
- *Assign a partner to help each student with a physical disability, if that seems appropriate.*
- *Give the student time to explain his or her limitations and needs (or take the time to do this yourself) so that other students are aware of what the student needs or appreciates.*
- *Be prepared for falls, and think about what you will do if this does happen: remain calm and let the student guide you into what kind of help is needed.*
- *Tape the student's paper to a table or lapboard to prevent slipping, and ask the student if he or she would like you to tie a string to a pencil and attach it to the table for easy retrieval if it is dropped.*
- *Provide a variety of learning activities that will encourage different responses.*

49

For those students with physical disabilities that you cannot see, such as allergies, be aware of any medications or special needs that may necessitate a change in lesson plans or use of certain materials. Especially with younger children, it is always best to check with parents or family members before offering the children a snack in class.

Students who are hearing impaired

There are many levels of hearing loss, and considerations for teaching will vary with each of these. In general, include the student who is hearing impaired in all activities by adapting the activities to fit each level of hearing loss. Some specific suggestions follow.

- *Talk with the student's family or other teachers for suggestions about teaching methods they have successfully used with the student.*
- *Realize that you may have to repeat and say things in a variety of ways before they are actually learned.*
- *Pair students together to help each other.*
- *Plan your seating arrangement in a circle or horseshoe shape so the student can see other members in the class.*
- *Seat the student away from other distracting noises, such as a window or furnace.*
- *Don't hide any part of your face when speaking to the learner, for example, putting your hand over your mouth. Be sure that lighting doesn't cast shadows that will prevent the student from lip reading.*
- *Use as many visual aids as possible, such as maps, charts, overhead transparencies, and others.*
- *Label shelves, books, and supplies in the classroom so that the younger student can become self-sufficient about locating or returning them.*
- *Face the student when you speak, and use as clear speech as possible. Incorporate body language and facial expressions into everything that you say.*
- *When presenting new language or terms, write them on the chalkboard or on an overhead transparency as well as saying the word clearly. If possible, check into having an interpreter in class.*
- *Begin to learn and use some basic phrases and words in sign language.*

Students with speech disorders

Students with speech disorders may or may not also have hearing loss. Students with speech disorders include students who stutter. Many of these students will be receiving therapy in other classroom settings.

Teachers who have a student who has a speech disorder can help them in these and other ways:

- *Show a caring, patient attitude in the class.*
- *Keep up with the flow of the conversation by giving your attention to the student as he or she speaks.*

- Let the class read in unison when asking for oral reading.
- Reinforce times when a word or phrase is used correctly.
- Provide opportunities for the student to be a part of nonverbal activities.
- Offer optional ways for the student to communicate, such as writing or typing.
- In a question and answer activity, record answers on 3" x 5" note cards so the student can point out the correct response.

Students who are visually impaired

The effect of visual impairment will vary from student to student. Advanced degrees of visual impairment can necessitate the use of special curriculum materials, such as large-print or braille. Other considerations in a classroom setting may include some of the following:

- The classroom should have adequate light with little or no glare.
- The classroom should be arranged in a consistent fashion. Let the student know if you move anything around.
- Keep classroom doors open or closed, but never halfway open.
- Use a heavy black pen to make worksheets or assignments.
- Record reading materials so that the student can listen to assignments that need to be read.
- Some students may benefit from a magnifying glass or magnifying page.
- Use concrete, tactile materials whenever possible to clarify verbal learning.
- Use verbal cues in lessons whenever possible.

Teachers who work with students who are blind should consider these suggestions:

- Say your name when you begin speaking until the student knows your voice.
- If the student would like, identify a partner to work with him or her as needed.
- Whenever possible, use three-dimensional materials such as relief maps. Locate braille or recorded materials whenever possible.

Students with A.D.D. (Attention Deficit Disorder)

Students who have A.D.D. do not have a behavioral problem, but a problem that is biochemical in nature. Some people mistakenly label A.D.D. as hyperactivity (which is, in reality, an effect of A.D.D.). Many gifted children are included in this grouping.

Teachers who work with a student who has A.D.D. can help them in the following ways:

- Build up the student's self-esteem and sense of worth in the classroom.

- Check with the individual student after giving the class directions for an activity by asking the student to repeat the directions.
- Depending on the age of the student, write the directions down or draw picture clues. A checklist of the steps to follow will help break the task down into manageable steps.
- Let the student sit near the front or near the teacher to prevent distraction.
- Consider putting the student in a more isolated area in the classroom to prevent distractions that might prevent him or her from following through on a task.

Students who are gifted

Students who are gifted or advanced need to have the opportunity to extend the learning to a higher level. Research and other advanced skills will challenge them, but keep gifted students in the same area that other students are in. Allow them to help the other students.

Jesus was the master teacher. We can learn much about teaching and learning by looking into the Bible at stories of Jesus' teaching.

People learn in many ways: by doing, by listening, by memorizing, by their mistakes, by correction, by punishment, by accidents, by failure, by watching someone else, by reading, by observing, by sharing, by repetition, by teaching. Just as there are many ways to learn, so also are there many ways to teach. This chapter will look at several things that result in successful learning. Not all methods or ways to teach will be addressed here, but enough information will be provided to help you make some choices about what kinds of teaching will work for you.

An effective teacher uses a wide variety of teaching and learning methods. Every method, when it is used in the appropriate situation, is good. If you know that you need to explore the use of new methods, allow yourself extra preparation time so that you are familiar and comfortable with the way you're doing something, and why.

Deciding on a method

Experts disagree as to the difference in the amount of information that is retained when it is taught with an emphasis on reading, hearing, seeing, or doing. There is agreement, however, that the greatest percentage of learning happens through *doing*.

Whenever someone is *actually involved* in the learning process, he or she will have the easiest time learning the information presented. If you have the choice when planning lesson activities, always choose a "doing" activity over one that is exclusively "seeing" or "hearing."

Consider these factors when choosing which methods are best for you, the children, and the material to be learned:

- *Lesson objectives.* What do you want the students to learn? Which method will bring this learning the most quickly?

- *Student behavior.* How do you want to affect the students' lives? Will the method you use help that? (For example, in a lesson that emphasizes cooperation, provide fewer scissors than the number of students in the class. How do they handle the problem?)

- *Lesson content.* The content of your lesson will help determine the method you choose to use. (For example, a lesson on the journeys of Paul could culminate in a map study, imaginary journal, or a study of missions today.)

- *Available resources.* Will you need special supplies or equipment for the method you choose? Be sure these are available to you and that you are familiar with using them.

- *Age and educational background of students.* Know your students! Make sure that you use age-appropriate methods and experiences your students can relate to their own lives.

- *Time and space.* Because some activities naturally take longer than others, be conscious of the time factor when choosing the methods or activities you will use in a lesson. Careful and realistic planning will eliminate frustration on both your part and the students' parts. What about the space you are meeting in? Some methods require movement and plenty of space to "spread out." Be sure you have adequate space for each activity, including a place to set aside materials, such as projects that may need time to dry.

Preparing the lesson

Lesson planning can be as easy or as complex as you make it. If you use a curriculum written especially for your grade level, you can have some confidence that the information, materials, and activities presented there are age-appropriate for the children in your class. But if you are planning your own lessons based on a theme or Bible story, you may need some guidelines to get you started in the right direction.

Here is a logical progression of the steps for planning a lesson for your Sunday school or vacation Bible school class. Even if you use a prepared curriculum, this information will be of help as you evaluate the curriculum materials and resources you plan to use.

Know your materials

To the best of your ability, know your materials before you enter the classroom to teach your students. Take advantage of introductions and overviews in books and other materials you are using as resources. Be sure to talk with other teachers who are using the materials you are or who have taught with these materials before. If you are planning your lesson around a particular theme or Bible story, check Bible resources such as a commentary for more in-depth information that you can use when planning around a text.

In addition, be familiar with both teacher and student resources that you might be using, including any activity sheets, maps, charts, or other visual materials. Check for the availability of equipment that you might need (such as a video cassette recorder and screen) and familiarize yourself with the operation of any of this equipment.

The "rules" of learning

While learning is a complex event, consider these "rules" and think about how observing them would affect your classroom.

- *Learning can be like a chain. All learning is connected in some way to previous knowledge or experience. One way of understanding learning is to break it into steps.*
- *All that takes place in a classroom should be a learning situation, not a testing situation. Avoid using activities that make students feel socially, academically, or emotionally uncomfortable. By assessing the students' learning styles and your own teaching style, you can match activities to the information to be learned and guarantee the students' success.*
- *The learning activities you choose should be true to the teachings of the Bible and the doctrines of your church.*
- *Choose activities that will help you to reach your goal or objective the most quickly.*
- *Choose activities that will contribute to the learning process, not merely those that are interesting or entertaining.*
- *Give your students the chance to think and decide on their own goals or on the course of action they will take. Give them choices and the freedom to make decisions within appropriate guidelines.*
- *When planning your schedule, alternate quiet and active kinds of activities to keep the students' interest and attention. This is especially important when working with younger children.*
- *Prepare your class for any new or unusual methods or activities that you will use.*
- *Encourage and welcome active participation and discussion in the classroom.*

Set goals and objectives

What goals or objectives are you trying to reach in this lesson? Do they match the activities you are planning, so that the learning takes place within the context of the information and experiences provided in the classroom?

Your objectives or goals will help you pattern the lesson in a logical and progressive way. Most teachers will try to balance the kinds of objectives around which they plan their lessons, including *cognitive, affective,* and *psychomotor* objectives (see sidebar). In addition, religious instruction also includes objectives that will help the students' faith development through both information and experiences.

What's the objective?

A balanced lesson plan contains different types of objectives. This ensures that learners will have the opportunity to learn on many different levels and in many different ways.

- **Cognitive objectives** *are those that involve recalling or remembering (knowledge), understanding (comprehension), using the information learned (application), making relationships with information learned (analysis), reassembling information and using it in a new situation (synthesis), and making judgments based on the information learned (evaluation).*
- **Affective objectives** *are those that involve feelings, attitudes, values, and beliefs. The first level is where the student merely becomes aware of an idea, process, or thing (receiving). Then the student uses this information and does something about it (responding). When the behavior or information learned has worth to the student, the third level of affective objectives (valuing) has been reached. When the student can use the information and processes learned so far to form his or her own choices, the next level of affective learning (organization) has taken place. In the final level, when the internalizing process is complete, the information is recognized by the student's philosophy of life (characterization).*
- **Psychomotor objectives** *usually are part of a lesson, whether they are planned for or not. These types of objectives have the students follow a procedure that includes seeing a behavior and then imitating it (observing), following directions and sequences and attempting to do something (imitating), performing an entire sequence repeatedly to learn it (practicing), and perfecting the skill or sequence so that it becomes an "owned" skill (adapting).*

Words that will help you identify or write objectives include the following: *realize, recognize, celebrate, become familiar with, respond, understand, identify, show, tell, create, participate, learn, feel, express, discover, use, develop, share, review, or discuss.*

Readiness activities

Set the tone or feeling at the beginning of the class session so that everything that takes place leads to the Bible story or the learning you want the students to have. When the teacher is in the classroom and ready as the children arrive, the tone will already be in place. If possible, arrange some self-directed activities with which the children are comfortable (such as marking their attendance sheet, reading quietly, or adding a special drawing to a bulletin board), so that you can spend a moment or two with each child individually.

If possible, plan all pre-lesson activities that lead the students directly into the Bible story, and make sure that other classroom activities have that emphasis as well. (One example would be to offer playdough as the prelesson activity. Then, as you begin the lesson on the creation story, you can refer back to the things that the students created as they played with playdough earlier.)

The Bible story

In religious education, the use of the Bible story is central to any lesson planning you do, whether you are writing your own lesson or using one that is already written. It is important for the teacher to not only read through the curriculum and the writer's interpretation of the story, but also to read the actual Bible text and other resource books that will give clearer insight into understanding the story. As you read and reread the Bible story, think of creative learning activities or experiences that you can incorporate into your lesson plan from which the children will benefit.

A Bible story can be presented in any number of ways, from using puppets or a flannelboard to using a video cartoon. The important thing to remember is to vary the presentation style periodically. (Chapter 6 contains more ideas about ways to present Bible stories. See pages 69–71.)

Related activities

The activities that you choose to use within your lesson will be as varied as the students in your class. Make sure that you alternate and try different kinds of activities to keep the students interested and to reach those who may not learn well in a particular way. (Some activities require sitting at a desk and using a pencil and paper. Others require permission to leave the church building to take a nature walk in the park.) Use your own creativity in thinking of activities that will best meet your objectives of making the Bible story meaningful to the lives of the students in your class.

Make a point to include and incorporate activities that require a response from the students as well. These kinds of activities may include writing and sharing individual or group prayers, litanies, and projects.

Asking questions

Sometimes it is only when we go beyond who, what, why, when, and where that we can discover what someone has actually learned. In Christian education, it is important to go beyond these basic questions to see if the students have been able to transfer to their own lives what has been taught.

The kinds of questions a teacher asks usually relate to the objectives he or she has set as part of the lesson plan. Without a doubt, the easiest questions to ask are those that ask a student to recall factual information. This type of question relates to the first stage of cognitive thinking.

The hardest questions to ask (and for students to answer) are those at the opposite end of the cognitive scale: questions that ask a student to evaluate what he or she has learned.

Think about the kinds of questions you usually ask. Then consider these points as you think of ways to use new kinds of questions.

- Ask clear, specific questions. Use short sentences and terminology with which the students are familiar.

- Ask questions in sequence, building on one after the other.

- Direct questions to the entire class, not just one or two students. When a teacher singles out one student to answer a question, it lets the other students "off the hook" and they may not even listen to the answer to the question. A better way is to involve all of the class in answering the question, either by writing the answer down or by asking each student to whisper the answer to the person sitting next to him or her.

- Pause for several seconds after asking the question. Students need time to think through their answers. Pausing also lets the students know that you expect them to answer the question. Don't answer for them! Research shows that teachers consistently allow only half a second between questions and answers. Strive to allow at least five or six seconds for the students to respond.

- Help students expand on and clarify their answers. If they seem to be having trouble answering the question, reword the question or ask another that will help them get to that particular point. Also, it is important to ask questions that can have many different answers.

- Ask a variety of questions to allow many different students to answer. (For example, don't just ask, "What is this?" but, "What do you know about this?") When students believe that their thinking makes a difference and that you respect their ability to think, you will also have helped build their self-esteem.

- Ask the students questions that require them to make inferences. Lead them into answering questions by speculating or making judgments. (For example, say, "What do you think might have been some of the causes of . . . ?" rather than, "What was the main cause of . . . ?")

- Ask students to support their answers. Encourage them to follow up their answers with supportive thoughts or comments. (For example, "What are your reasons for thinking the causes were . . . ?")

- Ask the students to come to conclusions. Have the students bring all of their answers together by asking questions such as, "After everything we've discussed, what are the main causes of . . . ?" Then add, "Please explain your choices."

Asking better questions

In order to ask a better question, it helps to think about the different types of questions and their purposes. How do you make use of each style in your classroom?

Type of question	Purpose	Example
Memory	recall, repeat, define	"Who was the first judge of Israel?"
Translation	interpret, explain	"In your own words, why did Moses not want to go to Pharaoh?"
Interpretation	compare, conclude, summarize	"How would you compare the call of Moses and the call of Matthew?"
Application	interpret, explain, summarize	"What is an example of helping in your home?"
Analysis	interpret, explain, compare, conclude, summarize	"What evidence do you have that the Israelites were unfaithful to God?"
Interpretation	speculate, predict	"Suppose Jesus had not been baptized by John. What difference would it make?"
Synthesis	judge, value, choose	"What new things did you learn about faithfulness from the story of Ruth?"

Closing

The closing to your lesson is as important, or even more important, than the readiness activity is. Try always to pull the students' thoughts back to the Bible story or learning before they leave. Whatever they did last will be what they most remember.

Lesson planning pointers

Some teachers can read through a lesson once and feel totally comfortable in teaching it the next day. Others need to rewrite the lesson in their own notebook, adding or changing the things that they are not comfortable with.

It is important to use the method that works best for you. Some teachers use a highlighting pen and underline what they want to say or do in the session. Others may jot down key words on an index card and clip it to the book they are using.

You may want to use an actual lesson plan form and write up your plans, including objectives and related activities. Whatever you finally choose as your actual method of planning, don't forget that at some time your needs may change and you will want to adapt even your own technique!

Learning styles/teaching styles

In recent years we have learned a lot about the different styles of learning and teaching. People are born with their own preferences for methods of teaching and learning. That is not to say that a person is limited to just one learning or teaching style. Rather, a person naturally works and learns most effectively and enjoyably in the areas that he or she is most comfortable. The best combination in the classroom is when a teacher's style and a student's style complement each other to create a positive learning environment.

As the teacher, help to create this positive environment by gathering information about the best ways for you to teach and the best ways for your students to learn.

Observe the kinds of methods of teaching with which you feel the most comfortable. Then channel your instincts so that you use a variety of methods to reach the students. When you are aware of your own learning/teaching style, you have a good framework with which to work in your lesson planning and in the actual teaching you do in the classroom.

Observing and noting each student's learning style will help you understand each child better as both a learner and an individual. When a teacher can capitalize on a variety of ways to present materials that take into account the different ways that people learn, then lessons will become easier to teach and more flexible.

Learning styles

Here are brief summaries of the three basic styles of learning. When you determine what kind of learner you yourself are, you will have a better idea of why you teach the way that you do. The hardest students to reach may very well be those who have opposite learning styles to your own, but with conscious effort, you will be able to offer them appropriate learning activities in the classroom.

- ***The visual learner.*** *These learners depend primarily on seeing information. They probably see pictures in their heads, accomplish a good portion of their work independently, are good memorizers, have an excellent imagination, and observe details. You can help these learners by including plenty of pictures and other visual learning activities in your classroom.*

- ***The auditory learner.*** *These learners depend on their ears to receive and process information. An auditory learner has acute hearing and verbalization skills, follows oral directions easily and quickly, is quick to answer spoken questions, and remembers names and numbers very easily. You can help these learners by telling stories, tape recording and reviewing information, or playing word games when memorizing Bible passages.*

- ***The kinesthetic learner.*** *These students learn best by actually doing something, especially something that involves their muscles. Research shows that most boys are kinesthetic learners, although not every boy has this style. These learners tend to be restless and inattentive when they have to sit for long periods of time and may have trouble following directions. They may also have difficulty in learning to read and write. Help these students by providing hands-on activities and opportunities for physical movement.*

Learning activities and materials

We have noted a wide variety of ways to teach and learn, and with each different way are numerous materials that can be used as learning aids. Some of those materials will be discussed here. Be sure to keep your eyes open, too, to discover different ways to use the learning materials available to you.

Lectures

Many teachers teach only by the lecture method. While it can become boring to use this method exclusively, it can work for all ages with a little forethought.

Keep in mind the age of your audience when using the lecture for a presentation style in the classroom. Young children have a short attention span but they are honest about letting you know when they are through listening! Be brief, use appropriate and familiar language, and try to add variety to your voice and style when lecturing to these children.

When lecturing in a classroom of elementary-age children, try to find interesting ways to present information, showing the students how the information you are sharing with them relates to their own lives. These children are in the thick of the learning mode and will be especially fascinated by topics that interest them. Combine a lecture of no more than ten minutes with other learning activities. This will be of benefit to the entire class.

Students in junior high have spent a good deal of time listening to lectures. It may take the teacher's most creative efforts to make the lecture something they are enthusiastic about hearing! Be sure to use vocabulary that challenges them (does not talk down to them). Encourage their discussion and reactions to the information learned.

Speakers

Inviting guest speakers adds interest and a new perspective in the classroom. Speakers may want to dress in a costume or bring visual aids to help them in their presentation. Let them know the age range and capabilities of your students.

Inviting a guest speaker, be it a parent or someone from your community, is a great way to keep interest high and to help your students see that there are others who share in their values and beliefs.

Flannelboards

The flannelboard is an excellent teaching tool, and not only for preschoolers! Even adults can enjoy learning from a flannelboard presentation.

Flannelboard figures or pieces can be made from paper, fabric, coloring book, or magazine pictures, and many other items. To make these items stick to the flannelboard, glue or tape a small piece of felt, flannel, or sandpaper to the back of them.

Another fun way to make flannelboard figures is to draw or trace shapes onto a piece of heavy pellon interfacing. You can find interfacing in most fabric stores, and I have found that the most inexpensive kind really works the best. Outline the shapes

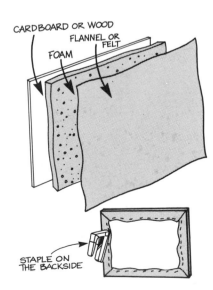

CARDBOARD OR WOOD
FLANNEL OR FELT
FOAM

STAPLE ON THE BACKSIDE

with a permanent felt-tip marker. Then color the figures with crayon or felt-tip marker. These flannelboard figures will not need a separate backing to make them stick to the board.

There are numerous ways to make flannelboards. Here are a few suggestions to get you started.

- *Cardboard or a piece of thin wood.* Cover the front of a piece of heavy cardboard or wood with a piece of felt or flannel, wrapping it around to the back sides. Staple, glue, or tack the piece so that it lays smooth across the front. To make the flannelboard even more usable, place a piece of foam or padding between the flannel and the board. Then you can also pin up items that will not stick to the flannel.

- *Flannelboard box.* Using a lap-size box with a hinged lid (such as a school box) makes a nice flannelboard and offers a storage place as well. Glue a piece of felt or flannel to the inside of the box lid. To use, set the box on your lap or on a tabletop and lift the lid, placing the figures on the felt as you tell a story. Store the flannelboard figures in the box when it is not in use.

- *Flannelboard lamp shade.* Use an old lamp shade as a flannelboard-in-the-round. Cover the outside of the shade with felt or flannel. The entire lamp shade can be set up with flannelboard figures, and if you have several "scenes" in the story, you can just turn the shade as you tell it.

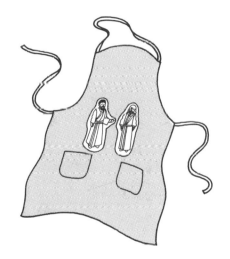

- *Flannelboard apron or skirt.* Use a skirt or an apron as a place to retell a flannelboard story by just placing the figures on the front as you tell the story. The pockets will make handy storage places for pieces not in use.

Magnet board

A magnet board is used in a way similar to a flannelboard. The equipment that works best to make a magnet board is a metal baking sheet and assorted small magnets or magnetic tape.

You can cut shapes or designs from poster board, magazines, or coloring books to use on your magnet board. Attach a small magnet or piece of magnetic tape to the back of each piece. Then use the shapes to tell stories.

Sand pan

A sand pan is another alternative to the flannelboard, and one that is especially fun for students to use with you. Fill a shallow pan (a cakepan or dishpan works well) with about one inch of

sand. Glue or tape craft sticks or pencils to the backs of the story figures, making sure that the stick extends about one inch below the figures. The figures can be moved around the sand pan with ease, but you may find that dampening the sand helps the figures to stand upright more easily.

This is a great method to use when retelling the story of Moses crossing the Red Sea!

Puppets

Many books and resources give puppet patterns and suggestions. Here are a few basic kinds of puppets you can make.

- *Finger puppets.* The simplest finger puppet of all is made by drawing a face on your fingertip with a fine-point felt-tip pen. A whole family of finger puppets can be made this way using only one hand! Add little paper hats from construction paper if you like.
- *Peanut puppets.* After a snack of peanuts, use the shell halves to make peanut puppets. Draw facial features and hair on the peanut shells with fine-point felt-tip pens and set the shells on the end of your fingers to tell the story.
- *Paper bag puppets.* Ordinary paper lunch bags can be used to make great puppets to use in class. Let children draw features and clothing on the front of their paper bags, leaving the bag flap folded over as the mouth. Construction paper features and yarn hair can be glued to the bag to add another dimension to the paper bag puppets.

  To use a paper bag puppet, slip your hand into the bag, curving your fingers into the folded flap. This becomes the puppet's "mouth" and you can move it open and closed to talk.
- *Shadow puppets.* Shadow puppets are fun to make with hands, cut-outs, and even with students! You must have a bright light and a screen made from a bed sheet or piece of white paper so that the shadows can be seen by the audience.
- *Hand puppets.* You need not be a master puppeteer to use a hand puppet. Young children especially respond to puppets and will look forward to hearing it tell stories or sing songs.

You can make a stage for your puppet show in a variety of ways. A tabletop or doorway can become a simple puppet stage, as can a box with a hole cut into one side. To make a doorway stage, make a single-casing curtain to fit onto a tension rod and fasten it into the doorway so that it hides the people behind it who are working the puppets.

A creative puppet stage for individual use can be made with a disposable diaper box. The handle makes the stage easy to carry. The precut opening (for removing the diapers) is where you put your hand through.

A more elaborate stage can be made with large cardboard appliance boxes or the boxes that bicycles come in. If you use an appliance box, cut a stage window opening and a doorway to allow the person controlling the puppets to step inside the box. Decorate the outside of the box if you like and add a simple curtain inside the window.

If storage space is limited in your room, consider making a collapsible stage. Once your puppet play is over, simply fold the stage flat and store in a closet or against a wall. To make this stage, you will need large pieces of cardboard. If you use boxes that bicycles come in, you will be able to cut them down to make four pieces of cardboard, measuring approximately 28″ x 50″ each. Cut the small edges of the boxes off. Then mark a 12″ x 14″ center window in one of the boxes. Score the top and bottom edges of the window and cut through them to make windows that will open and close.

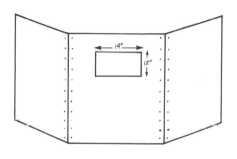

Punch holes along the vertical edges of the panels about 5″ apart. Do the same along one edge of two of the other cardboard panels and set the three panels into position. Thread them together with string loops as shown.

You can paint or cover the panels with self-adhesive paper if you like.

Electronic equipment

Electronic equipment is here to stay and can enhance the learning environment of your classroom. If you have record players, tape recorders, film projectors, or video equipment available to you, it is a good idea to check with your Sunday school superintendent or Parish Education Committee about the possibility of using this kind of equipment in class.

Students today are used to a variety of this kind of media and will look forward to its use in your classroom.

There are numerous catalogs available that have video and audio tapes for rent or for sale.

Cassette tape recorders can add a new dimension to many different parts of your lesson. Use them to prerecord music for singing, recording scripts to accompany puppet shows or other dramatic productions, recording the narration of a Bible story if you will be absent and will have a substitute, taping sounds for a sound game, or offering taped directions in a learning center. This is one piece of equipment that every classroom would benefit from having, and they are fairly inexpensive to purchase, as well as easy to use.

Teaching/learning activities

A general list of different teaching/learning activities is given here. As you read through the list, add to it your own ideas for new and different ways of teaching.

age-appropriate assignments	*flannelboards*
bulletin board games	*flash cards*
charts, posters, and maps	*games*
creative crafts and projects	*lecture*
creative writing	*magnet boards*
creative dramatics	*music*
debates	*puppets*
field trips	*sand pans*
films, filmstrips, or videos	*speakers*
finger plays	*worship*
	and many more!

Teaching options

Many congregations are finding that they need to reassess how they conduct Christian education in their churches. The most common and well-known way of teaching has been to have one teacher and one grade together in a class. With today's life-styles, this doesn't always work.

Many options are available that will help make the classroom a more vital and positive place. In some cases, this may mean that Parish Education Committees and Sunday school superintendents will have to rethink the ways that they recruit and supply teachers for the classroom. Consider these options.

- *Group grading* is used in many Sunday schools that have a limited number of students. In a group-graded classroom, students of several grades are grouped together in one room, and use the same materials. The teacher makes necessary adjustments in how the material is presented or used to fit the reading and writing abilities of each child.

- *Team teaching* allows teachers to work together, either sharing in the classroom preparation and activities each week or by alternating weeks or responsibilities. This arrangement can allow flexibility for teachers who want to take part in the church's adult education programs or for times when a teacher may be absent on a Sunday. Husband and wife teams may enjoy working together in this way.

- *Learning centers* work well when students are of different ages or abilities. In a learning center classroom, many different interest areas are set up and students work independently. Usually, the teacher presents the basic Bible story to the entire group, then gives the students time to reinforce the theme by allowing them to choose which centers they will work at during the remainder of class time.

- *Intergenerational classrooms* are another popular way to teach, especially in a smaller congregation or on a periodic basis when a change is needed. In this type of classroom, all ages of learners participate, and the activities are adapted within the groups so that everyone benefits from them. In groups like this, older and younger participants can teach and learn from one another.

- *A semester system* allows an opportunity to alternate the teaching staff. Many people might be more willing to teach if they had some flexibility for scheduling, including the opportunities to be involved themselves in Bible study or adult classes during the education hour. Churches that use this system do have to recruit twice as many teachers, but they often find that more teachers are willing to return year after year because they don't get tired of teaching for an entire year.

Your church's Sunday school program operates in order to provide opportunities for learning. Think about some of the teaching methods discussed in this chapter. Then exercise your flexibility and ingenuity in meeting your own needs, as well as your students'.

Telling a good story is an art that not everyone has, but it is one that most people can cultivate. There is nothing quite like the rich simplicity of a Bible story to demonstrate to us how much God loves us.

Everyone has his or her own story to tell, and most people will eagerly tell you about themselves and their lives. Although teachers can easily tell their students about something they have done the day before, sometimes they don't think they are qualified to tell a Bible story in the classroom. But with thoughtful practice and an understanding of basic storytelling techniques, many people can comfortably tell a Bible story.

Tell a story

Before you begin thinking about how you will tell a Bible story, choose a story from the Bible. Read it over to yourself several times. The first time that you read it, become familiar with the details in the story. On your second read, ask yourself, "What does God say to me and to other people in this story?" The third time you read it, think about how you can present this story to the children in an alive and interesting way.

Storytelling

Jesus told many stories to people in the Bible, and it can be helpful to examine those passages to see how he told stories. Usually the stories that Jesus told were simple stories without many details. The stories also related to something within the hearer's experience. We need to remember these points in our storytelling because the simplicity and relevance of the stories that Jesus told were what made those stories so important to the people who heard them.

Another part of our preparation for storytelling should be to think about the different parts of the story and what we want each of those parts to do for the learners.

Most stories have a similar form: a beginning, development, the climax, and the end. The beginning is the setting of the stage—preparing the hearer for the upcoming story. Step two is the development of the story. Characters and plot are introduced and students are drawn into the story.

The development of the story leads right into the climax or high point of the story. Often in a Bible story, this is the point where a character realizes that God is central to life, or a time when God actually intervenes in the life of the character.

The end is just that—the ending of the story. When telling a Bible story, the end is a good time to state or restate a central truth that ties up the story or makes a point that the learners can take into their own lives.

Now you are ready to think about how you want to present a story to your class. Consider ages of your students. Remember that older students enjoy drama, excitement, and action in stories as much as young children. They can often see humor in situations or comments that younger children can't.

When choosing your storytelling method, make the story come alive. Maintain eye contact with the students, using your facial expressions and tone of voice to bring the story to life.

How to tell the story

Bible stories can be told or retold in a variety of ways, ranging from puppet shows to teaching posters. Consider some of these ideas to enliven your retelling:
- *Make a story strip viewer (like a television). Cut a viewing window in a box and wind a picture strip through it.*
- *Use a flip chart with story pictures.*
- *Use flannelboard figures (see pages 62–63 for suggestions about making a flannelboard).*
- *Tape record sound effects to enhance your storytelling.*
- *Dress up as a story character and tell the story from your point of view.*
- *Make a story jigsaw puzzle from a picture that is central to the story. As you tell the story, add one piece at a time, saving the last piece for the end.*
- *Use a "mystery box." Fill it with objects that relate to the story and pull them out as the story is told.*

As with any learning activity, the visual images you use help to make the learning significant and more meaningful to the learner. (Bringing a fishing net into the classroom and pretending to pull it into a boat is one way to help students remember the story of Jesus and the fishermen, for instance.)

After you have told the Bible story, involve the students in activities that relate to and follow up on the story. Anytime children actually experience something that relates to the learning, their retention will be increased. This is truly active learning! Some ways to do this include the following: discuss the story; pantomime or act it out; dress up; pretend to be a character who talks about the story or writes a journal entry reflecting their version of the story.

The whole purpose of good storytelling is to excite the students with the story so that they will be eager to share it with others. Although they may not rush right home and tell the story, it will come out in their words and actions.

Reviewing Bible stories

Here are some fun ways to review Bible stories and memorize verses or other things. Be sure to try several and add your own ideas when planning and working with the children in your class.

- *Make a Bible story scrapbook.*
- *Act out the story with simple props and costumes.*
- *Make word picture cards. Scramble them and have students recall the story as they put them back in order.*
- *Retell the story with a flannelboard.*
- *Write riddles that use three or four "clues" so that students can guess the name of a story character or place.*
- *Play a review game of "20 questions."*
- *Play charades with Bible characters or story events.*
- *Have students draw or paint pictures to illustrate their favorite story scene from a Bible story.*
- *Work on a group mural that shows the sequence of story events.*
- *Play a "hot potato" review by sitting in a circle and tossing a ball to different people. Each person will need to contribute the next event or fact about the story.*
- *Put together a "round robin" review sheet. Each student writes down the next event in the story.*
- *Make storybook review banners with pennant-shaped paper and hang them from the ceiling. Let the students use their favorite story as the basis of their banner.*
- *Write and illustrate a class newspaper to tell stories the class has read or learned about.*
- *Play an alphabet game. Ask the students to think of objects from the Bible and have them fill in the object at the end of this sentence, using the letters of the alphabet as a guide. For example, the first player might say, "I'm going on a trip and I'm going to take an apple." Have the students identify the story their word comes from.*
- *Write biblical "Who am I?" riddles and exchange them with each other.*
- *Write a script for a Bible story and do a puppet play using your script.*

- *Make symbol banners that represent your favorite Bible story. For example, a banner about Noah could include an ark, a rainbow, water, and a dove.*
- *Write a letter to a Bible story character, asking questions that weren't answered in the story. Then have the students exchange papers and answer each other's questions.*
- *Scramble the words in a Bible verse and challenge teams to put the verse together correctly.*
- *Make a Bible quilt from paper squares (or fabric using fabric crayons) to reflect favorite Bible stories or to show scenes in a particular story.*

Using your memory

Sometimes it's not clear just what to have the students in our classes memorize, or why. Is it really important? How can we fit it into an already full schedule? What about children's varying abilities?

My views on memorization have changed in the past few years, or perhaps my methods and expectations of memorization have changed.

Children's minds are very good at learning and memorizing things that they hear repeated often. Children can and do memorize every day: songs, advertising jingles, corporate logos. We ought to also give them the opportunity to memorize important things that they can carry with them the rest of their lives.

One of the best ways to help children memorize is to set the words to music, rhythm, or rhyme. A clapping rhyme is a good way for a three-year-old to learn a simple Bible verse. When we can see, hear, and say something, we are engaging more than just one sense. Chances are good that we will remember more when we learn in this way.

Furthermore, when children see that what they learn or memorize is relevant to their lives immediately, they will be more eager to learn it. Some of the things that we should be having our children memorize, then, include simple Bible verses (including the text references), songs and hymns of our faith, poems or other inspirational words, and parts of the liturgy or worship service that is used in our congregation. It is especially important that they learn and memorize parts of the liturgy or worship service so that they truly feel like part of the community of believers. If we want them to continue to worship regularly after they have passed the school-age years, they need to feel connected to the church and its rituals.

Creative learning activities are any activities that enhance the student's ability to think and allow them opportunities for self-expression. In religious education, these kinds of activities can be key to the growth and nurturing of a student's faith.

This chapter focuses on some specific ideas to help you plan and use creative, hands-on learning activities as part of your teaching. This is a starting point. Always keep yourself on the lookout for other books and activities that will be something you and your students may enjoy trying in the classroom.

Art projects

God spent time creating the world and everything in it. As people created in God's image, we too are interested in creating things. Children enjoy creating, and teachers should encourage them in whatever ways they can.

Children have great imaginations and when they are encouraged to search for solutions to problems in the process of creating, they will discover many things about themselves. There is more than one way to do each project. Allow each child to discover his or her way of doing that one thing.

One caution: it is easy to get caught up in the end product rather than in the process. When working with children, we need to focus more on the entire process that they are exploring and experimenting with. We should be more concerned that they have an opportunity to try new things than that they produce a perfect product that can be displayed on a refrigerator!

Here are some fun and easy ideas for art projects to try in your classroom. These can be altered in a number of ways and each child's own creativity will produce different results. You may want to have available materials for two or three projects at the same time so that students can choose an art medium to express themselves.

Crayons

Crayons can be used in several different ways in artwork. Try one or more of these.

- *Crayon "stained-glass" windows.* Have students draw their window designs on white paper, then draw over their outlines with ink or permanent black felt-tip pen. Use crayons to color the spaces in the design. Turn the paper

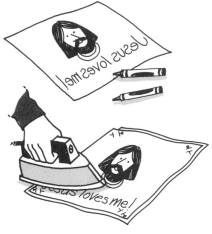

SANDPAPER

NEWSPAPER
PAPER
SANDPAPER
DRAWING

over and rub it gently with a piece of cotton or toweling dipped in vegetable oil. As the paper dries, it will appear transparent and the colors will seem brighter. When hung in a window the light shines through the "stained glass" and resembles a stained-glass window.

- *Waxed paper and crayon melts.* Grate old or broken pieces of colorful crayons or candles using a cheese grater. Sprinkle the crayon shavings between two pieces of waxed paper in a pleasing design. Then sandwich the waxed paper between sheets of newspaper. Iron the sheets firmly with an iron (set on warm). The iron will melt the crayon shavings into a design and fuse the two pieces of waxed paper together.

- *Quilt squares.* Using fabric crayons, draw a design on pieces of paper. (If there are any words, be sure they are written backwards so that they appear right when printed.) Pin the paper with the design to a muslin or other plain fabric square and press with a warm iron, transferring the design to the fabric. Use the squares to make a quilt or other fabric item.

- *Crayon resists.* Have the students color a picture using heavy, dark crayon. Then "wash" over it with watercolor or tempera paint. Any spaces that are not covered with crayon will pick up the paint but the waxy crayon portions of the picture will "resist" the paint.

- *Hot wax drawings.* This is a fun project to try with older children. You will need a food warming tray or an old electric frying pan with a "low" setting. Lay a piece of aluminum foil on the tray. (Set the pan on low.) Use crayons to draw a design on the foil. The low heat setting will make the crayons melt as you draw, creating a nice, flowing design. Remove the foil when you are pleased with the design and let it cool.

- *Sandpaper prints.* Have students draw a bright, colorful design on a piece of sandpaper. (Make sure that they color hard with the crayon as they will be transferring their design onto paper.) When they are pleased with the design they have drawn, place the sandpaper on a piece of paper and sandwich both between several thicknesses of newspaper. Press with a warm iron. The sandpaper design will print onto the paper, creating a picture that has "dots" from the sand. These make great note or greeting cards.

Printing

Printing can be done with any number of objects. The best paints to use are tempera (or poster paint) and acrylic paints. Both are

74

water-soluble and nontoxic. Printing can be done on any kind of paper, cardboard, and even some fabrics when they are fastened to a firm surface underneath. Try printing with some of these objects:

> corks, either plain or with designs carved in them
>
> cookie cutters
>
> erasers with designs cut into them
>
> potatoes and other fruits or vegetables
>
> foam packing materials, either glued to a wood or cardboard block or cut into designs
>
> string or rubber bands attached to wood blocks with double-stick tape
>
> sponges cut into shapes and clipped with a wooden clothes-pin
>
> anything else that strikes your fancy!

Paint possibilities

It can be difficult to paint in a short period of time, such as most Sunday school classes have. Painting is very rewarding for children, however, and is worth the extra effort to give it a try. Here are some ideas to try:

- *Dry tempera.* Have students dip their brush or cotton swabs in water, then in dry tempera paint to paint on paper.
- *Colored pencils.* When the ends of colored pencils are dipped into water, they produce a paint-like effect and can be used to draw with.
- *Finger painting.* Use one of the recipes on page 79 and try finger painting. Glossy shelf paper is best for finger painting, and taping the paper to the table will make it easier for the children to use.
- *Straw painting.* Mix paint and water to a thin consistency then drop paint spots onto the paper. Use a straw to blow the paint into designs.
- *String painting.* Fold a sheet of paper in half, then dip a length of string into paint. Lay it between the folded sheet of paper, and gently pull the string through from one end to the other. The string and paint will make a swirl effect on the paper.
- *Sponge painting.* Use sponges clipped to wooden clothes-pins to paint.

"Big pictures"

- *Murals.* Make a mural as a class activity. Use a large sheet of shelf or butcher paper, divided into enough spaces so that each student has one to work on. Murals are a good way to review a story or draw a creation scene.

- *Montage.* A montage is made by combining a number of different pictures or symbols together to create one larger picture. Use magazine pictures, old calendars, catalogs, or other pictures to create a thematic montage.
- *Collage.* A collage is similar to a montage, but it is made by combining a variety of materials. Some collages center around one color and incorporate as many different things of that color as possible. Paste and heavy paper, such as poster board, work best for making collages.
- *Mosaic.* A mosaic is made by combining many small things such as pieces of paper or even eggshells to create a picture or symbol. A montage differs from a collage in that the picture is drawn on the background and then filled in with the pieces.

Using art with children

Consider these things when doing art with children.
- *Children draw, paint, and create from their own observations, knowledge, and experiences. Respect their individuality!*
- *Through their artwork, children assimilate their environment and relationships to it. They also organize it and begin to determine new relationships based on what they know. Encourage this exploration process.*
- *When children create, they share in God's creation. Value this gift and teach them to value this gift in others.*
- *Children tell stories through their artwork. Invite them to share their stories with you and with others.*
- *Through their artwork, children give from their innermost selves. With their permission, display their work so that other people can enjoy it too.*

Artistic development in children

Artistic development in children shows itself in four basic developmental stages. Use these guidelines to help you plan the artwork your students will do.
- **Scribbling period (ages 2-4).** During this period children will move from making random marks on paper to more controlled and repeated motions. If a child places a name or identity on a drawing, write the titles on the paper along with the child's name and age.
- **Pre-schematic period (ages 4-7).** During this stage of development children begin to use symbols that represent certain ideas or feelings that they want to express. Space is an emotional experience, observable by objects in pictures that may seem to "float" on the

page. This is how the objects appear to the child. Color choices are also emotional and children draw only the parts of objects that are important to them. Thick paint, crayons, and clay are the best materials to offer to these children.

- **Schematic period (ages 7-9).** *Children of these ages use their art to communicate their ideas and feelings. Pictures often begin by showing realistic space with ground, air, and sky. Children express what they know, not necessarily what they see and will still continue to exaggerate the things that are important to them in their drawings. Children in this developmental stage also are more aware of themselves in the total world. They may draw "x-ray" pictures that show both the inside and outside of something, serial pictures that show the development of action and multi-perspective pictures that will show many viewpoints at one time. Introduce and let the children use more of a variety of materials for their artwork.*

- **Dawning realism period (ages 9-11).** *For most children, this period is a time of discovery in nature, geography, science, and art. Art begins to reflect more details and realistic colors. Figures of people and animals may seem to be more "stiff" because children try to include all of the detailed segments; or some children may leave figures out of their artwork altogether because it is too "difficult" for them to draw. Children in this age range begin to have a perspective on space and will overlap objects on a page. More sophisticated methods are tried with different materials, and this age group likes working in groups.*

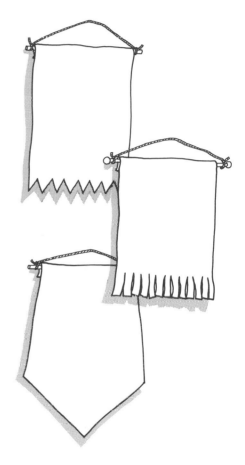

Banners

Banners can be made from a variety of materials. Felt and burlap are good choices when working with children. They don't require hemming and can have items glued to them. Banners can be any shape or size. They usually contain a saying or words of some kind, as well as symbols or a design. The diagrams on this page present several ideas for banner shapes.

Yarn and starch drawings

Dip assorted colors and kinds of yarn into liquid starch. Then lay it on poster board or cardboard in a pleasing design. When the starch dries, it is clear.

Mobiles and stabiles

Mobiles and stabiles are a popular item for all ages to make. Mobiles hang from the ceiling and usually contain many different elements. One example would be to use a Bible story as the basis

for a mobile and have students create items to add to the mobile that serve as a review of the story characters and events.

One of the problems with mobiles is in balancing the items so that they hang evenly. Use wire clothes hangers, dowels, or even paper plates as the mobile base. Paper plates can have holes punched around the edge with yarn tied through them to attach the items.

Stabiles are similar to mobiles except that they stand on a table or the ground. A can or bucket filled with sand or stones can hold a dowel or tree branch steady so that the stabile stands straight.

Dioramas

Dioramas are made in small boxes, usually a shoe box. They are stand-up scenes that show a story or event. A small eye hole is cut into one side of the box to "peek" through.

Chalk drawings

Chalk is an interesting medium to work with. Usually, chalk drawings look best when done on dark paper.

- *Wet paper chalk drawings.* Dampening a piece of paper before drawing on it with chalk will cause the colors to appear brighter and more exciting when they dry. To make non-smearing chalk, add six to eight tablespoons of sugar to about one inch of water in a pan. Mix well until the sugar dissolves. Soak the chalk in this for 10–15 minutes. Then allow the chalk to dry before using it.
- *Sidewalk chalk.* Use chalk to create a sidewalk mural. When you are finished, the sidewalks can be sprayed clean with water.

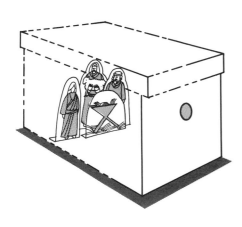

Sand paintings

Have the students draw their designs on a sheet of heavy paper. Then have them fill in their design with white glue. Spread or sprinkle colored sand over the glued areas, shaking off the excess. Set them aside to dry.

To color the sand, shake dry sand with dry tempera paint in small jars until you achieve the color you want.

Masks

Children love to dress up in disguises! Simple masks can be made from construction paper and used to retell Bible stories or role-play contemporary stories.

Show the students how to draw a large mask shape in the center of a 12″ x 18″ sheet of construction paper. Add large tabs to the edges of the masks. Then cut them out and add decorations with paper scraps or felt-tip pens. Crease the tabs at the sides of the masks and fold them back, overlapping them so that the mask is curved. Glue or staple the tabs.

Recipes

Finger paints

Finger paint #1
   1 c. flour
   ¼ c. salt
   2½ c. cold water
   food coloring
   Combine all ingredients and blend with a mixer while heating the mixture over medium heat. The mixture will become thick and clear. Add coloring of your choice and a few drops of a preservative such as oil of cloves or wintergreen.

Finger paint #2
   liquid starch
   dry tempera paint
   Pour liquid starch on glossy paper and sprinkle dry tempera paint over the starch. Finger paint!

Finger paint #3
   1 c. liquid starch
   6 c. water
   ½ c. nondetergent soap chips
   tempera paint (liquid or dry)
   Dissolve the soap chips in the water until there are no lumps. Mix well with the starch and add dry or wet tempera paint or food coloring to get the colors desired.

Play dough

"The Best"
   3 c. flour
   1½ c. salt
   6 teaspoons cream of tartar
   3 c. water
   3 tablespoons cooking oil
   food coloring
   Sift the dry ingredients into a sauce pan. Mix the liquids and add the coloring. Blend all ingredients well and cook over moderate heat, stirring until the dough pulls away from the pan or when it can be squeezed without feeling sticky. This mixture stores indefinitely in an airtight container.

Uncooked dough

2 c. flour
1 c. salt
½ c. water
food coloring
Mix the ingredients in a large bowl. Add the food coloring of your choice. Extra flour may be needed to prevent sticky hands and tabletops.

Play clay

1 c. cornstarch
2 c. baking soda
1½ c. cold water
Mix the ingredients well and cook over medium heat for about four minutes, stirring constantly until the mixture thickens. Cover with a damp cloth until it cools, then knead. This play clay will harden and can be painted with tempera, watercolor, or acrylic paints. Spray or dip the completed pieces in clear shellac to preserve them.

Play dough to eat

½ c. peanut butter
¼ c. honey
1 c. dry powdered milk
Mix the ingredients (½ c. of the dry milk) in a bowl with your clean hands. Keep adding the remaining dry milk until the dough feels soft, not sticky. Have the children wash their hands, mold, then eat and enjoy!

Paste

Paste is a good art medium to use, especially with younger children.

Quick paste

Add a little water to ½ c. of flour and mix to a thin paste.

Cooked paste #1

Mix equal parts of flour and water to a thin paste. Boil slowly for about five minutes, stirring constantly. Cool and thin with water if needed. Add a few drops of oil of cloves or wintergreen as a preservative and store in a covered container.

Cooked paste #2

1 c. flour
1 c. sugar
4 c. water
1 teaspoon alum
2 drops oil of cloves
Mix and cook in the top of a double boiler, stirring constantly until the mixture thickens. Beat the mixture with a rotary mixer while cooking to prevent lumps from forming. Store in an airtight container.

Creative writing

Your students can use writing to express thoughts, feelings, and ideas. When using creative writing projects and activities in your classroom, be sure to let the students have the freedom they need to express themselves. Some children will work better individually while others will prefer working on writing projects in small groups or as a class.

Try some of these ideas to get students thinking about how they express themselves through writing.

Acrostic poems

Acrostic poems are poems based around a certain word. For example, using the word *thanks,* one sentence or thought is written for each letter of the word. The only rule is that the sentence must begin with or include that letter. Here is an example.

T - Today is the Lord's day!
H - Happy are God's people.
A - All joyfully celebrate.
N - Noisy cymbals and clanging gongs,
K - Kids of all ages together.
S - Sing together, family of faith!

Haiku and Senru

Both haiku (HI-koo) and senru (SEN-roo) are forms of Japanese poetry that are very much alike in their form, although they differ in function. Haiku represents a single thought as it relates specifically to nature. Senru represents a single thought on any subject.

The poetry form is made up of three lines. Line 1 has five syllables. Line 2 has seven syllables. Line 3 has five syllables.

One example is:

One tiny raindrop
spattering on a green leaf.
Drip, drop, drip, drop. Plop!

Cinquain

Cinquain (sin-CANE) is a French word that means "group of five" but a cinquain is also an American form of poetry.

The form for a cinquain consists of five lines. Line 1 is the title (one word). Line 2 has two descriptive words. Line 3 has three action words. Line 4 has four words that express a feeling about the title. Line 5 is a synonym of the title (one word).

An example of a cinquain is:

Jesus
kind teacher
loving, giving, caring
shared God's good news
Lord

Prayer poems

Prayer poems can take many different forms and are a combination of poetic style and words that express prayer thoughts to God. These can be written individually, in small groups, or as a class. One thing you might consider doing with class-written prayer poems is to share them with other members of your congregation through a newsletter or weekly bulletin. Sometimes a pastor or worship leader might even use one of your prayer poems in the worship service.

News report

Have students take on the role of a news reporter, either with newspaper, radio, or television reports. These can be written or shared with the class as a way of reporting or reviewing a Bible story or other activity. An "on-the-spot" reporter can interview a character from a Bible story and help the students to get a different perspective of the story and what meaning it can have on their lives.

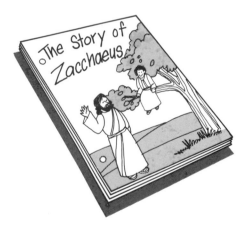

"Big" Bible storybooks

Older students can write and illustrate "big books" that can be shared with the church library, with younger students, or even with a preschool or day-care center. To make a "big book," use two sheets of poster board for the cover, stapling or punching holes and using brass fasteners or rings for the binding. Let the students design and illustrate a cover. Then have them rewrite or retell the Bible story in simple terms that younger children can understand. Be sure they add an illustration to each page.

Class newspaper

Help the students design and write a class newspaper that they can share between themselves, with other Sunday school classes, or even with a church in another city. Be sure to include photo or illustration space and consider printing up copies of the newspaper with a computer or typewriter so that it has a professional look. Some things to include in the paper are stories about what you have been doing in class, cartoons, Bible story activities (such as puzzles), and anything else of interest to the students.

Paraphrasing Scripture

One way for students to become more familiar with Bible stories is to have them paraphrase certain Bible passages or stories. By writing the stories in their own words the students will have a chance to think about the significance of these stories and Bible truths in their own lives.

Journal writing

Journal writing is an especially good way to help students write about their feelings, thoughts, and ideas. If setting aside time for journal writing during class time is not possible, encourage the students to take a few minutes during each day to do so at home.

Finish the story

When presenting a new Bible story or a contemporary story to the class, read only to a certain point and then ask your students to complete the story. This can be a fun and enlightening way to take the students to the next level of learning for that particular story, and the discussion that follows is sure to be lively!

Graffiti wall

Provide a space in the classroom or somewhere else in your church where "good" graffiti about God and God's love can be written. Encourage everyone in the church to participate in this activity by adding favorite Bible verses, "bumper sticker" sayings, and original drawings to the wall.

Drama

An ancient Chinese proverb says:
 Tell me, I forget.
 Show me, I remember.
 Involve me, I understand.

 This explains why using creative dramatics in the classroom is so important. If our goal is to make Bible stories and Bible learnings relevant to the lives of our students, then we need to remember to involve them in as many different ways as possible.

 How often do you use drama in your classroom? Read through the following descriptions and decide on some methods to try with your class.

Mime

The word *mime* means "to imitate." In mime, actors use motions, rather than words, to share an experience with the audience. Mime is a very expressive way to portray events, thoughts, and feelings because it involves the observation skills of the audience in such a vital way.

Have students mime everyday activities, animals from creation, even people from Bible stories. Be creative about using mime yourself to get the students' attention during class activities or storytelling.

Charades

In charades no words are used, although some people do allow the use of sound effects. When using charades, the actor is trying to get the audience to guess what he or she is doing or who he or she is.

A fun way to use charades is with a Bible story review. Write a name and text reference on a small piece of paper. Then give one slip to each student. Let them act out their story for the rest of the class with everyone guessing what Bible character or story they are representing.

Frame drama

A frame drama is like watching a slide show. Actors are "set" into still scenes and no narration or dialogue is used to tell the story. Instead, at a given signal like a bell or hand clap, the actors move into the next still scene.

Creative dramatics

Most people have not had a lot of experience with creative dramatics and may feel a little uncomfortable when asked to "act it out." Keep the following points in mind as you begin to incorporate drama into your lesson plans.

- *Enjoy the process! Don't worry about producing something "perfect."*
- *Establish a classroom climate that makes the students feel comfortable and secure.*
- *Be enthusiastic about taking part in the drama activities.*
- *Be prepared that the first class attempt at drama may not be perfect.*
- *Set guidelines that the students know and understand, such as "Respect what others try to do."*
- *Use drama activities often so that students feel comfortable participating.*
- *Encourage as many students as possible to participate. Sometimes you should ask for volunteers. Sometimes you should assign parts to encourage the quieter students. But don't pressure anyone to take part who may not want to.*
- *Always include follow-up discussion after drama activities.*

Echo pantomime

In an echo pantomime, the leader tells a part of the story using actions. Then the students repeat that same phrase or sentence with the actions, and so on, back and forth. Many times, rhyme or repetition is a part of an echo story.

Choral reading

In a choral reading, groups are assigned parts (such as "Group A" and "Group B") and alternate telling parts of the story aloud. Because all of the students are involved in telling the story, their retention is usually greater.

Role play

Role play is different from other kinds of dramatic readings because there is no script for the actors to follow. Usually the actor or actors are given a situation and then they must react to it as the character they are playing.

This works well with contemporary stories or life situations, as well as Bible stories. One benefit of using this type of drama is that the students are in a position of finding a solution to a problem or a situation.

Music in the classroom

Not everyone thinks that he or she is capable of singing with students in a classroom. There are ways to help yourself become more comfortable. Music can be incorporated into your lesson planning in such a way that everyone, including the teacher, will benefit.

A teacher needs to guide and direct the children's singing so that participating is a joyful thing, not one of stress and anxiety. Whether you think you can sing well or not, you can help your students enjoy music together.

Preparation is the key to making music in the classroom a joyful experience. Rather than relying on your own music skills and capabilities, your enthusiasm is what will make your students the most responsive when participating in classroom music time. View yourself as a participant as well and you can then relax and concentrate on the music, the words, and the interaction the children have with one another.

It isn't necessary to play an instrument to be a song leader for children. Remember, your voice is your own musical instrument!

Choosing songs, hymns, and music to use with the students in your class is an important task. Because children have distinct periods of development in their musical abilities, as well as in other areas of growth, it is good to keep some of the following guidelines in mind. With all young children, it is good to include songs that have repetition, short simple verses, strong rhythm, and clear rhyming patterns. Finger plays or other actions combined with music can help some students who have a more active learning style.

The quickest way to learn songs is to follow the printed lyrics as you sing. It is important for teachers to memorize the words to the songs they sing with children because you will need to be free to help children and interact with those who may need it.

Selecting music

Use the following guidelines to help you select music that your students will enjoy.

- **Two- and three-year-olds.** *Look for songs that are repetitive, can have the child's name inserted, combine simple finger plays with the music, echo songs, and songs with actions.*
- **Three- and four-year-olds.** *These children need songs that have more complex actions, include more complicated echo parts, involve counting, and introduce or reinforce simple concepts.*
- **Four- and five-year-olds.** *These children want to sing even more difficult songs (like songs that have several simple verses) and like complex action and drama songs.*
- **Five- and six-year-olds.** *Choose songs that play with words and sounds—even silly rhymes—in addition to the types of songs enjoyed by younger children.*
- **Six- and seven-year-olds.** *At this age, children like to join in singing simple rounds, enjoy songs that tell a story, like more complicated action songs, enjoy songs that continue to add verses or concepts, and want to sing songs with a wider voice range.*
- **Eight- to ten-year-olds.** *Continue to add lively songs that include a wider voice range and have actions. In some cases, the song that is sung faster for this age group is definitely better! Songs that have accumulative stanzas are usually enjoyed by the children in this age group as well.*
- **Ten- to twelve-year-olds.** *These students' voices may be beginning to go through some changes. They are not as eager to sing the songs they have been learning all along. Be aware of current types of music (the rap style is one example) and let the students be involved in adapting these kinds of music to other songs about Bible themes, or even writing songs of their own. Accumulative songs are still a good choice and adding new verses or stanzas is fun for everyone in the class.*

By incorporating music into your curriculum and lessons on a regular basis, you will be adding yet another dimension to the students' learning.

Making music

Your classroom can be a place for music, whether you consider yourself a musician or not. Following is a collection of ideas for ways to enhance your classroom learning with music.

- *Old tunes—new words.* Choose simple children's songs that everyone knows, such as "Twinkle, Twinkle, Little Star" or "Jesus Loves Me." Then create your own words for the songs. The children will especially enjoy doing this as a class!
- *Scripture chants.* Speak the words to a Bible verse in a rhythmic chant. Then try to add clapping rhythms. This is a good way to let everyone in class join in music. Chanting can be less threatening to both teachers and students and may give them the confidence to sing.
- *Portions of worship.* It is important to teach children portions of the liturgy, the benediction, and other parts of your church worship service that are sung or chanted. This will help children to participate in worship and know that they belong at the services. Ask a music director or choir director at your church to help you choose certain portions to teach to your class.

Instruments to make

- *Sticks.* Attach ¾" dowels (approximately 7" long) together with eye screws and a string.
- *Gong.* Drill holes and attach a handle to a baking sheet as shown. Then use a lollipop stick and a rubber ball for the mallet.
- *Drums.* Drums can be made from any round tins or boxes. Various sizes and those made of different materials will make different sounds.
- *Scraper sticks.* Notch a 1" dowel in an even pattern on one side. Then use a smaller dowel to rub against it.
- *Sand blocks.* Glue sandpaper to paint sticks or any paddle-type piece of wood. Rub them together to make a sound.
- *Wrist bells.* Attach jingle bells to a piece of elastic and sew the ends together into a bracelet. Make one for each wrist.
- *Jingle.* Attach different sizes of buttons to a clothespin or dowel, using a flathead nail to pound into the top. The buttons will rattle together loosely.

STAPLE EDGES...

OR TIE WITH YARN

- *Maracas or shakers.* Put small pebbles, popcorn, or paper clips into the opening of an aluminum soda can. Tape the opening shut and shake. Make shakers with a variety of different items so that they all have a different sound.
- *Tambourines.* Put dried beans or pebbles between two paper or aluminum plates and staple the edges together. Another method is to lace the edges together by punching holes in the edges and threading yarn through them. Add ribbon or crepe paper streamers if you like.
- *Bells.* A table fork or spoon suspended from a piece of string can be struck with another fork or spoon to make a bell-like sound.

Evangelism and outreach

Evangelism and outreach are so interrelated to Christian education that these topics could easily fit into many different sections of this book. Generally, children will draw adults to church through their involvement in activities, by their performances, and by adults who want to share in the faith lives of their children.

Following is a list of things some churches do to reach out to people in their communities. I hope that you will find at least one new idea here that you and your Sunday school can try!

- Serve a light breakfast of juice and muffins. Encourage families to come together and allow parents time for fellowship while the children are in Sunday school.
- Send personal invitations to the people that you know, or even those that you may not know. Announce the start of new classes and provide information on learning and worship opportunities for the whole family.
- Offer vacation Bible school. This is a great time to include visitors.
- Have several events during the year when people of all ages can participate in learning together. Seasons such as Advent and Lent easily lend themselves to this kind of event.
- Have a yearly slide show that features the kinds of activities people in the church are involved in.
- Have an open house where parents can meet teachers and visit classrooms.
- Send home a newsletter on a regular basis that tells what kinds of things you are doing in class.
- Send a newsletter to kids in the neighborhood that invites them to Sunday school. Also, offer ideas of things they can do.
- Plan an event such as a picnic or swimming party and encourage the students to invite their friends and neighbors.

- Join together with other classes and work together on a mission project, either in your community or somewhere else.
- Plan together to visit and share worship with residents of a care facility, such as a nursing home or day-care center.
- Encourage the students in your class to think of the kinds of things they would like to do to share God's love with other people!

Worship in the classroom

Worship is an important but often neglected part of class time. Some teachers are not comfortable leading worship because they think that they are not qualified to do so. But anyone can be a participant in a time of praising, singing, and worshiping God.

One important factor to consider when including worship in your lesson planning is this: the attitudes and experiences that children have in classroom worship will transfer to their involvement and attitudes toward congregational worship.

A classroom worship service has four basic parts: readings, prayers, music, and offerings or gifts. We will look at these parts individually and offer ideas you can use in your own class.

Prayer

Prayer is many different things, not just requests for things that we may want. Prayer includes praise, adoration, thanksgiving, confession, and intercession.

Teach your students that God is always ready to listen to and answer our prayers, but that sometimes those answers will not be what we want or expect. We cannot expect God to do everything we wish. But we do have the assurance that God will always be with us and will help us in all situations.

Sometimes praying in a new way can help us experience new things. Try to introduce your students to some of the following prayer methods.

- *Five-finger prayers.* Teach your students to use their fingers as reminders of the basic parts of prayer: praise, adoration, thanksgiving, confession, and intercession. Their five fingers can serve as reminders of different things to include in their prayers.

  Or have the students use their fingers as prayer reminders. The thumb can be a reminder to pray for friends and families. The index finger is a reminder to pray for the people who point us to God (like pastors, teachers, and parents). The middle finger is the tallest so it can remind us to pray for the people who are leaders in our

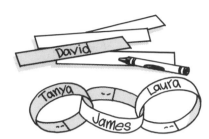

cities, states, and countries. The ring finger is the weakest finger on our hand and can remind us to pray for people who are less fortunate than we are. Finally, the littlest finger can be a reminder to pray for ourselves.

Using either of these prayer methods will help your students get past the "gimme prayers" that are so easy to pray.

- *Prayer chains.* Make paper prayer chains as prayer reminders. Cut 1″ x 6″ strips of construction paper and give several to each child. Let the children write their prayer requests or the names of people they would like to pray for on the strips. Then attach them together in a loop.

  Connect all of the students' strips together into one chain for the class time of prayer. Or let the students make individual chains to take home and use there.

- *Prayer poster.* Make a theme prayer poster to use as a central part of your class worship. One example of this is to use pictures cut from magazines, words, or drawings the children have made about the things they are thankful to God for. Glue these things on a large sheet of paper in a montage effect and center your time of prayer together around it.

- *Prayer journal.* Encourage the students to keep their own private prayer journal, recording the dates and prayer requests that they make. Then have them record the times and ways their prayers are answered.

- *Prayer litanies.* Work together as a group to write prayer litanies that can be used in class or even in your church worship service. A litany can be written with several parts, perhaps one that is repeated often and the other being read by a leader or smaller group. Gather the students' ideas on a chalkboard or large sheet of chart paper to make it easy for everyone to follow along.

  Following is an example of this.

Leader: We thank you, O Lord, for life, for fun, for friends, and for families. O Lord,

Group: We thank you!

Leader: Whenever we are sad or lonely, we remember that you are with us. O Lord,

Group: We thank you!

Leader: Above all we are grateful for the gift of eternal life that we have through Jesus, your Son. For this great gift, O Lord,

All: We thank you!

Music

Read through the "Music" section on pages 85–88 to get ideas of how to incorporate music into your classroom worship.

Offering or giving

It is only appropriate that we should give back with grateful thanks to God who has given us everything. When your attitude of thanksgiving is joyful, the children will learn to also be joyful in their giving, both to God and to others. Here are some ways to make the offering or giving part of classroom worship even more meaningful.

- *Group project.* Encourage the students to think about and discuss where they might want to give offerings taken during the class worship time. Is there a local food shelf that would benefit from a donation? How about a day-care for underprivileged children? A missionary that is sponsored by your church?

  When the students have the opportunity to choose where they want their monetary offerings to go, they will be more excited about the possibilities and realize that their gifts can make a difference.

- *Poster or scrapbook.* Make a class scrapbook that keeps track of the kinds of things your class or Sunday school does as part of their offering back to God. Take pictures, keep statistics, and give regular reports to the Sunday school and to the congregation as well, so that everyone can celebrate the joy of giving.

- *Love coupons.* Help the students realize that their gifts or offerings do not always have to be money, but that the gifts of love, kind acts, and thoughtfulness are valuable too. Help them to make "love coupons." Use 3" x 5" index cards to write or draw what they will do as an act of love for someone else. Coupon books make especially nice gifts during the holidays or at special times.

- *Offering containers.* Make the taking of the offering a fun thing in your classroom by relating it to the seasons of the year. For example, use a plastic pumpkin to collect the offering during the month of October or an Easter basket during the month that Easter occurs.

  You may also want to relate the container to a specific mission project. For example, an offering for world hunger could be collected in a bread bag.

"And whatever you do, whether in word or deed, do it all in the name of the Lord Jesus, giving thanks to God the Father through him" (Colossians 3:17 NIV).

And whatever you do. . . . Hopefully this book will serve as a guidebook for you to accomplish what God has called you as a teacher to do. You can help God's Word become more real to the children you teach. You can assist students as they struggle with the faith questions of today. You can make the lives of people of the Bible serve as examples of what our lives can be like with God's help.

I hope that when you consider your calling as a teacher, you will look first to the Bible and then to this book. My goal is to make the real "nuts and bolts" of teaching accessible to everyone, and to help teachers see past the scissors and glue and glitter. Remember, you can make a difference in the lives of God's children.